ONLY IN AMERICA

The Story of the
Alessio Brothers

by Angelo Alessio

as told to
Mike MacCarthy

Sunbelt Publications
San Diego, California

Only In America

Sunbelt Publications, Inc.

Copyright ©2003 by the author
All rights reserved.
First edition 1999 by San Diego Writers' Monthly Press.
Second edition 2003 by Sunbelt Publications.
Edited by Jane Firstenfeld
Book design by Leah Cooper
Project management by Jennifer Redmond
Printed in the United States of America

Sunbelt Publications, Inc.
P.O. Box 191126
San Diego, CA 92159-1126
(619) 258-4911, fax: (619) 258-4916
www.sunbeltpub.com

06 05 04 03 02   5 4 3 2 1

Library of Congress Cataloging-in-Publication Data

Alessio, Angelo, 1917-
    Only in America : the story of the seven Alessio brothers / by Angelo Alessio; as told to Mike MacCarthy.-- 1st ed.
        p. cm.
    Includes index.
    ISBN 0-932653-53-7
        1. Alessio, Angelo, 1917—Childhood and youth. 2. Italian Americans—California—San Diego—Biography. 3. Alessio family. 4. San Diego (Calif.)—Biography. 5. San Diego (Calif.)—Social life and customs—20th century. I. MacCarthy, Mike. II. Title.

F869.S22 A44 2002
979.4'985052'0922--dc21

                                                        2002012084

To Dominic and Rose

Acknowledgements

To all those who encouraged and helped me write this,
my first book, and especially to:
My wonderful wife, Mardy; Sam Ellis;
Judy Knight; Victor Mature; and Rosalie O'Brien.

Author's Note

Today as I begin to write this book, it's April 15, 1998. I've never attempted anything like this, and my heart is filled with many conflicting emotions. Telling our family story has been a project I've dreamed of for a long time.

Before my brother John died earlier this year, I tried to get him to help me. He kept saying I'd make a fool of myself and the rest of the Alessio family. He worried about family secrets, though I reminded him that since all our secrets were already in the media, my re-telling them really wouldn't make any difference. Besides, the truth is the truth.

Sadly, I never did convince him, and now I'm the only living member of the first generation of San Diego Alessios left to tell the real story. It's a story of struggle and of success. I hope those who read it will find it both interesting and inspiring.

Some who pick up this book will feel they know us already: the Alessio name has been in the public eye for many decades. Some who read this actually will know me, my brothers or our offspring. But I am moved to write this book because what you read in the newspapers is not always the whole truth, or even the unvarnished truth. I'm writing this because I want the world to know what we did, and how we did it, as told by someone who was really there, who really lived it, and who helped make important decisions in the past that still influence San Diego today.

Our story is in some ways a typical American success story, centered on the seven sons of Italian immigrant parents who rose from desperate poverty to financial heights. We started with no money, no connections and little education.

Most of us never even finished grade school, but at one point we owned several blocks of downtown San Diego real estate. We participated as major players in local, state and national politics, and even internationally, working in tandem with the Mexican government. We became major stockholders in one of San Diego's largest local banks, and owned or controlled some of the most successful businesses in all of southern California. Those achievements are what make our story extraordinary.

✦

I've always been a shutterbug, and I've got boxes of photographs stored in my office, home, and garages. They've served to refresh my memory as I prepare to write this book, and I hope you, too will find them an interesting glimpse into the past. They are tangible evidence that the Alessio saga was not just a dream or the wishful thinking of this old man.

I also keep a photographic "gallery" in my house. There are only about four good pictures of just the Alessio brothers. My favorite was taken when we took control of Tijuana's Caliente racetrack in 1947. That one puts a lump in my throat, even a few tears in my eyes. Those were great days for the Alessios, and I miss them still: my brothers, my parents, those magical days when we were still young, having fun, and working hard to make our dreams come true.

The story you're about to read is the truth. Maybe you've heard other stories, other versions of these stories. Whatever anyone may say to the contrary, this is the truth as I remember it. I was there, and I'm still amazed.

Part I

The Early Days

CHAPTER ONE

Across the Atlantic:
Southern Italy to West Virginia to Southern California

The history of the San Diego Alessios began as a love story in a remote Italian village more than a century ago. There, in a hamlet called San Giovanni in Fiore in the rugged Calabrian Apennines of Cosenza province in the far south of Italy—in the ball, if you will, of the Italian foot—our parents Rose and Dominic were born, courted, and married.

Dominic was barely 20 when he left Cosenza in 1900 with his brothers Antonio and Frank. They arrived, flat broke, in West Virginia, where they sought work in the coal mines. Antonio soon left for South America, another favorite destination for Italian immigrants.

Dominic and Frank stuck it out in West Virginia, first in Berryburg, where they escaped a disastrous mine fire, and later (joined by Rose) in Harrisburg. Eventually, Dominic and Rose settled in Clarksburg. By then, my eldest brothers Frank and Russell, though barely teenagers, were considered old enough to work in the mines, but our father saw to it that they never did. Instead, Frank and Russell went to work in a local pottery plant.

I myself was too young to remember much about our life in West Virginia, but I'm told it was a do-it-yourself existence. Anything we wished to consume we grew or raised ourselves. We usually had two hogs in the backyard that we'd butcher in November, when it was cool enough to preserve them without refrigeration.

My brothers remembered this as a festive occasion. The family would make a day of it and the neighbors would pitch in, too. The younger kids would help the neighbors catch and tie the hogs, which weighed 300 to 400 pounds.

Then by tradition, Frank, the oldest brother would stick the hog in the throat and bleed it. The pig would be deceased by 7 a.m., but the butchering process took all day. The blood was drained into a bucket, which was put on the stove and stirred up with walnuts, raisins and chocolate, to make Italian *sangguinacci*—blood pudding. I hear it was delicious.

So, while the women made blood pudding in the kitchen, the men would hang the pig on a specially made brace and start carving. Much of the hog became sausage. Casings were bought in advance, and everyone helped to cut up, grind and stuff the sausage. Even though I was only two or three at the time, I do remember the tasting part. I remember, too, that we shared not just the sausage, but pork chops and other goodies with the neighbors. That's the way it was in those days. We shared the labor and we shared what we had.

The Alessios, circa 1920

CALIFORNIA BOUND

Relatives and neighbors did stick together back then. As our family grew, so did my mother's workload. By 1919, Rose was the mother of seven boys, from newborn Tony to Frank, a healthy 16-year-old. Frank was by then providing much of the family's support, because Dad was mostly incapacitated with asthma. Lung disease from his years in the mines surely contributed, but his asthma must have been genetic. I, too, alone among his sons, have suffered from asthma all my life, though I grew up in sunny southern California and never set foot in a coal mine.

To cope, Mom took in boarders—as many as 15 at a time, this in addition to us nine Alessios. Twenty-four people in one house meant an amazing amount of work, and Rose did it all by herself. She fed us, washed our clothes, did the sewing and the cleaning. She baked bread. And still, she found time to volunteer as a midwife for other relatives and neighbors. Like I said, people stuck together then. That's so important to remember.

Finally, though, Dad was so sick that there was no alternative but to try a better climate in California, and those relations came through for us. They brought my father what they could, and persuaded that proud and apparently physically robust man to accept their help.

We left West Virginia on the train in 1921, with a little more than $400. Just imagine: my mother, her wheezing husband and their seven sons, all starting a new life 2000 miles away, on $400.

The Alessio luck was with us, though. When we arrived in San Diego at the Santa Fe Station we were met by a gentleman from the Garibaldi Association, an Italian benevolent organization. He helped us get situated in our new hometown, but still, it was a struggle.

CHAPTER TWO

Dominic and Rose Alessio, a Strong Foundation

y mother never looked at calendars. She didn't understand
them, and, of course, she couldn't read English. In fact, until the
end of her long and eventful life, Rose never was comfortable
speaking English. My mother communicated with her family in her own
distinctive way.

For example, it took me years to discover my actual birthdate by
contacting the West Virginia recorder's office. My mom always remembered that historic date as "stormy, train went off the track," near our
West Virginia home. Of course, since I was next-to-the-youngest kid,
my birthday was not as memorable as Johnny's seven years earlier. He
was born the day of the big West Virginia coal mine disaster.

Rose ran the home, but despite his delicate health and his prema-
ture demise, my father was a powerful figure in the lives of his family.
He was a good man, a hardworking man, and we brothers revered him
almost as if he were a saint. As you'll see, he set us all on the path of
ambition and hard work that has served the Alessio family so well.

He was a big man, a disciplined man, and a disciplinarian, too.
After we moved to San Diego, he rarely left the house unless he was
dressed in a suit, tie, and hat. Though he had no education, his native
intelligence allowed our big family to get by on almost nothing. He got
me and my brothers working at an early age, and that served us and the
whole family very well.

When he died in January of 1933, I was not quite 16 years old.
Tony was almost three years younger. But we and our older brothers
were already on the path Dominic had set for us.

It must have been a year until Dad's death was not the first thing on my mind when I woke up every morning. For Mom, though, it was so much harder. She had known him all her life, borne him seven sons, crossed an ocean and a continent with him. How sad it was to see her, years later, sitting on the porch, rocking on her chair, tears flowing down her cheeks.

She was a giant of a woman, over six feet, and strong in every way. She was Dominic's woman, and when he was gone, no one ever could replace him. But, for her sons, she kept on, and for that we were so thankful.

How strange it must have been for her, in later years, to live alone! I'd visit her frequently at our family home on Wabash Avenue, and as soon as I'd walk in the door she'd ask "Angelo, do you want some spaghetti?"

"No, that's okay, Mom. You don't have to do that."

"Oh yes, yes, I'll make it, I'll make it now," she would insist. "Sit down!"

Well, you can't say no to your Mom. And cooking came so naturally to her. She never measured anything, and I don't know how she made her sauce, but I know I'll never taste anything as good as that again.

Of course, that great heart had plenty of room for her daughters-in-law and her grandchildren. Our wives would drop in and find Mom wearing old, darned together socks. Each of them would go out and buy new socks, and next time they came by, Mom was still in those raggedy old socks.

Where were the nice new socks?

"I'm saving them," she'd say, but she never went anywhere. She'd rock on her old-fashioned porch swing, and wait for some company, even if they spoke only in English. Neighbors would drop in every day, and if she liked them, she'd give them loaves of the fresh bread she still baked in her outside brick oven at 2 a.m..

This woman, unschooled, from the poorest part of Italy, who crossed half the globe to be with her husband and raise her sons, who never spoke the language of her adopted country, our mother Rose, she was something special. She didn't often speak of "love." She lived that word for all her family.

She was so strong, so kind, and so loving. Such a good cook! We never really knew all that she went through, because she was always doing for others, always doing for "her boys"

Mom died at Mercy hospital in 1955, having survived her Dominic by 22 years. She was 77 years old, with diabetes and heart problems. Even so, in the weeks she was there, the nurses would comment, "Man, I've never seen a woman like that! "

And really, nobody ever had.

CHAPTER THREE

Welcome to San Diego:
Shelter and Food

The first challenge facing the Alessio clan upon our arrival in San Diego was finding a place to live. We had little money, no local knowledge, and our parents barely spoke English. And there were nine of us.

After a few short-term stays, we found a place on Wabash, half a mile from the city dump, in what's now the City Heights neighborhood. Then, as now, it was a wonderfully mixed neighborhood, with families of many varied origins. The kids from these families would turn out to be my best friends, and their parents, the best friends to our family. From the beginning, those wonderful people helped my mother, her ailing husband and her seven boys, including baby Tony and myself, a three-year-old toddler still wearing dresses.

It's a good thing the neighborhood was friendly, because the house itself was cramped, to say the least. Somehow, in no more than 800 to 900 square feet it contained three bedrooms, a single bath, all nine Alessios and a boarder, Benny Oliverio, whom I believe had been friends with my parents since Italy.

(l-r) rear: Benny Oliverio, Frank, Angelo
front: Tony, John, Ray Bond, Joe

One bedroom was for the older brothers. Frank and Russ shared a double bed; Louis and John another, and Benny Oliverio slept on a cot. Joe, Tony and I shared a double bed in a second bedroom, really only half a room, curtained off beside the kitchen. Mom and Dad had a bedroom to themselves.

Once we had rented this house, my father built an outdoor brick oven, where once a week, Mama baked fresh bread. Other Italian families also shared the oven, so the neighborhood was often perfumed with the irresistible fragrance of baking bread.

When Mom baked, we boys in the our curtained-off bedroom would be awakened at the crack of dawn as she mixed the dough next door in the kitchen. Next, she'd go outside to stoke up the dome-shaped oven with wood my brothers had pre-cut and stacked. While the oven was heating up, Mom would clean and wash it, then test it by tossing some dough inside. If the dough turned dark too fast, the oven was too hot, and Mom would open the portholes in the side to cool it off. She sometimes would have to repeat this process several times until the temperature was just right. She'd make 12 or 15 loaves each time, each of them three or four pounds.

Finally, the scent of baking bread would wake up the rest of the family, and everyone would be up and waiting for the first loaf to come out. We didn't have butter in those days, so Mom would spread on olive oil, a custom that has recently become popularized again in fancy Italian restaurants. And why not? It's delicious.

Good food is so important, especially for a family of growing Italian boys. Even in that tiny house, there was room for a special closet in which we stored that home-baked bread to keep it from getting hard and stale before next baking day.

Even though by 1920 the city of San Diego had a population of 74,361, much of the surrounding area was still undeveloped. We lived within two miles of Mission Valley, at that time mostly small farms and dairies and no paved roads. Sometimes on Sundays Dad would bring us boys down there to the tomato fields. They'd already been picked over two or three times. All that remained were the culls. We'd pick those leftovers, bring them home and dump them into big tubs in the backyard.

We'd help our mother fill a tub with water and pick the best tomatoes for sauce-making. She'd get up early the next morning and clean them, then bring them into the kitchen and start cooking. It was a messy, steamy operation. When the tomatoes were all cooked, she'd seal them up in Mason jars and store them in the basement.

We'd also drive out to olive orchards, where my father would ask the rancher if we might collect the olives that had fallen to the ground. Most were really ripe—pretty black, but we'd bring them home along with the green ones. After we washed them, my mother would cut them in her expert way, throw in some herbs, put them in big five gallon crocks, cover them with a board and weigh the board down with heavy rocks. This is how we made that rich olive oil to flavor our home-baked Italian loaves.

What else was on our table? Well, it wouldn't be an Italian meal without wine, would it? There was a little garage attached to our house and that was the Alessio Winery. Like the tomato sauce and the olive oil, the raw ingredients were also scrounged from nearby farms. We'd find a small vineyard, wait until the crop had been harvested once or twice, then Dad would buy the rest of the grapes for almost nothing.

In the garage, there was a big, round vat set about two feet above the ground. Below the vat, an open barrel. We'd dump the grapes in the vat, and then Joe, Tony and me, the three youngest kids, would get in the vat and dance around and stomp those grapes, while the juice seeped through the porous bottom of the vat and into the barrel. It was a lot of work. Well, it was a lot of exercise. I don't recall that we minded, too much, 'cause we got to eat all the grapes we wanted.

And because, with all those people and a single bathroom, we didn't get to take too many baths, we kind of relished that, before the grape stomping began, we had to get our feet really clean. Of course, with all that grape juice under our toenails, it took almost another year to get them clean again.

The wine was fermented in five-gallon barrels, and stored with the canned goods in the basement.

In this way, the traditional Italian cuisine and culture became part of our new lives in San Diego. At dinnertime, we sat in birth order at the table, and we'd eat lots of spaghetti with Mom's homemade sauce, and bread baked in our own back yard. And we boys, too, would drink that rough red wine that we stomped with our own six feet.

Bringing Home the Bacon

Now we had a place to live, and wholesome food on the table. But the family needed money for the rent, for clothes, for transportation. Although our father was in delicate health, he was sharp. He had a magnetic personality, and presented himself as a gentleman. And although he had no formal education, his native intelligence put the family on the path to survival, and eventually, success.

Almost the first thing he did when he arrived in San Diego was to get a job cleaning the pool hall at Imperial and 25th. Immediately, he delegated this work to his eldest sons.

Next, he went downtown to a barber shop at 8th and Broadway, then the hub for San Diego shoppers. There, too, he made a deal with the owner. He (and, of course, his sons) would keep the barbershop clean for free, in exchange for one chair where "his boys" could shine shoes.

The owner took him up on the deal, and Louie, the third brother, was put in charge. At a second location, next to Lyons Clothing Store at 5th and E, another central San Diego location, Dad secured another shoe shine stand. That's where he put John to work. John, the fourth brother, had to quit school in seventh grade.

Off to School

While the four elder brothers willingly went to work to support the family, they all agreed that the three youngest, Joe, Tony and myself, should go to school and get as much education as we could. So, when I was four or five years old, I was enrolled at Edison Grammar School at Polk Avenue and Wabash, only a couple of blocks from our house. Joe was four years older than me, and he went there, too.

Our mom made our clothes for us, and she bought the cheapest fabric she could find. I vividly remember the orange and white checked cloth she made my shirts from. With our used or hand-me-down pants and our wild colored shirts, Joe and I took a lot of abuse.

"Here come the dagos, the Italian dagos!" our schoolmates would yell.

I didn't try to fight back or punch them out, because I didn't think what they were saying was that important. I wanted to keep them as friends, and I didn't want to cause trouble.

We Italians weren't the only ones to suffer what would today be considered racial harassment.

Many of our neighbors had black skin, and in the 1920s, most white people in San Diego called black people "niggers." Coming from West Virginia, I'd never experienced this. It was wrong, of course, but it was just common practice for that time and place.

I can say I don't think I was ever a racist myself. Around the time I started school, we had a black family living next door, and the daughter, Ellen, was a little older than me. She was a real cutie, and I fell in love with her. The whole Edmonds family became close to the Alessios. The father worked in the commissary for the Navy at

Mrs Edmonds and Rose Alessio

North Island, and somehow he often managed to bring home hams and steaks of the best quality, which he'd share with us. Ellen and her sister were always well dressed, and we thought them quite well-to-do.

The Edmonds helped our family add a screened bedroom to our house, so Dad would be able to breathe more fresh air for his asthma. Sometimes during the night he'd be struggling for breath, and Mrs. Edmonds would see the light come on. Like my Mom, she was a big woman, more than six feet tall. She'd come over and try to help my Dad get more comfortable. That's the kind of friends they were. In our racially mixed neighborhood, this kind of acceptance was the norm.

So when we'd get hassled at school, it wasn't such a big deal. But there was one thing I really hated about our name: it started with an "A."

The teachers would seat their classes alphabetically, and I was always right there in the front row. I was a great talker, and I was always getting in trouble, 'cause I had nowhere to hide. The good thing about school was that my little neighbor sweetheart Ellen was in my class, and would help me with my homework.

Even back then, I was a flirt, and I'd ask the teachers if I could help them out. I'd tell them how nice they looked—and they swallowed it! I was kind of cute, I guess, with curly black hair and a big personality, but like my dad, I had asthma, and that made it harder.

And we were different from most of the other kids. Everyone else would bring a bag lunch to school, but Joe and I had to walk home for lunch. We'd get hard cheese from the icebox, and some of Mom's good bread. We'd heat up a little olive oil and dip in the bread. Sometimes I'd even sneak a little glass of wine.

Like most kids, I hated being different, and once, when I just couldn't take it anymore, I stole some lunches. The next day, the teacher announced "We have to put a stop to this lunch stealing. We'll catch the person sooner or later." That scared me enough that I never did it again.

HOMEWORK NO GOOD

After that, I kept my nose clean and put it to the grindstone. It was hard to do well in school, because our parents didn't realize how important an education was. I'd bring home schoolwork, and Mom would just look at it and say, "What is that, home-a-work? Home-a-work ain't-a no good!"

Our folks wanted to put us to work as soon as we got home from school. Dad laid down the law, "Get home right after school." He didn't mean ten minutes later.

When we got home, our chores were waiting. Tony was too small, and the older boys were working at their jobs, but Joe and I would go out in the backyard and start planting seeds or pulling weeds. We always had a vegetable garden, and we grew what we needed to eat and put in spaghetti sauce. While the kids up the street were playing, we were helping our family survive.

Interestingly, one of my favorite forms of recreation, both as a kid and as an adult, also helped put food on the family table. Paul Parson, who lived across the street, had a successful auto repair shop on 16th Street, and sometimes he'd pay me 10 or 15 cents to help him repair Dodges, his specialty. Maybe that's why, when I was around 12, he offered to take me fishing.

He had a boat and a motor, and he took me to Otay Lake about once a month during the season. I knew nothing about fishing, but he was a good teacher, and fishing has remained a pleasure all of my life.

Chapter Four

My High School Career

Our older brothers had only gotten through fifth grade, but Joe and I stayed in school and eventually graduated to Woodrow Wilson Junior High. It was much farther from home, but we still had to walk to school. Usually, we left home without breakfast, but we always had coffee. Sometimes Mom would buy corn flakes and we'd have a special treat: corn flakes mixed with coffee.

By now Joe and I were doing odd jobs and making enough so we could actually buy our own shirts. No more "dago brothers" specials. We didn't own an iron, so I'd press my pants under the mattress every night to get a crease. If I made as much as a quarter, I'd turn it over to Dad to help with the household expenses, but he'd give me a nickel back and then I could have a school lunch, another rare treat.

I still wasn't a great scholar, and I still was getting along by flattering my teachers. Woodshop was my favorite class, and I made many things for my parents.

In Biology we sometimes had field trips, and one fall I got tripped up by our Italian ways. We had just made our annual batch of wine at home, and as always, after the wine was pressed, there was a residue left over. These skins and grape seeds are called the "lees." We'd burn some of the lees in our fireplace, but we always had too many, so Joe and I would have to dump them someplace. This year, Dad suggested we dump them behind the high school.

Now, grape remains rotting in the hot San Diego sun create a pungent aroma. Imagine my chagrin when our junior high Biology class took a field trip behind the high school.

My classmates started yelling "Those Italians, those dagos!" I didn't say a word, but eventually they figured out that we had done it. Sometimes it seems my school career was just one long embarrassment.

EARLY BRUSHES WITH FAME

One great, enduring memory of those days was making friends with a boy who grew up to be one of baseball's greatest legends. Ted Williams lived a block from our house, and after we met in junior high, we played ball together whenever we could.

He was always over at our house, a nice guy, and kinda skinny. My mother loved him, and always tried to fatten him up with some of her home cooking or pastry. Her strategy never worked, though. Throughout his glorious major league career as baseball's greatest hitter, Ted was known as "The Splendid Splinter." Our friendship has lasted all our lives.

Around this time, my father struck up a friendship with another Italian fellow named Albert. Albert was the personal valet, cook and gardener for the movie actress, Irene Dunne. The elegant and witty Miss Dunne had been a musical star on Broadway before she moved to Hollywood in 1930. She is not so well known today, but she starred in many classic pictures, most memorably, several with Cary Grant. She was nominated for five Academy Awards.

Albert was a classy guy and a talented chef, and he had considerable authority at Miss Dunne's estate. Every six months or so our family would go up to Hollywood to visit Albert. It was quite a big deal for us to visit a movie star's house, but we couldn't stay overnight, so we'd drive up and back the same day.

Later, Miss Dunne bought an orange ranch in Corona as her summer home, and assigned Albert to take care of that house. Albert spent most of his time there, and sometimes when Miss Dunne was not in residence he'd invite us up to spend some time. We'd take the five hour drive in our old Studebaker, and I'd bring my BB gun. I don't think Albert was married, and he didn't have any kids, so he more or less adopted the younger Alessio brothers.

We'd really live it up at the Corona ranch. It was a huge, two story house with about 12 bedrooms, furnished with beautiful antiques. We didn't spend too much time inside, though. Albert had his own quarters; he'd make us huge meals and we'd stay up all night. Then he'd get us up early and we'd go hunting. Many rabbits lived in the orange groves; Dad brought his shotgun and we would hunt and eat them, a traditional Italian delicacy.

Extra Curricular Activities

Even though all the Alessio brothers had our household chores and our outside jobs, we still tried to participate in school activities. I played baseball with Ted Williams, and basketball, too.

Joe was very involved in theater productions. One time he went out to collect some greenery to decorate the stage. He came back with armloads of an attractive, shiny green plant. He was so proud of himself, and was happily dressing the set, until someone advised him he had bushels of poison oak. Poor Joe ended up itching with the worst case of poison oak I ever saw!

Fortunately, in those days doctors made house calls. Our family physician was a Dr. Ratty, who'd taken a liking to my father and went out of his way to take care of us kids. His office was about three miles east of us on Fairmont Avenue, but he was always at our house when we needed him.

Except for when I had a school check up and was told I needed to have my tonsils out. Dr. Ratty was too expensive, so Dad went and found a man who said he'd do the job at the house.

I don't know what exactly his qualifications were, but apparently he was not a doctor. Fortunately our neighbor Mrs. Edmonds was there during the operation, because, when the operation was only partly finished and I was still under the ether, the "surgeon" got scared and told her, "I'm through."

He walked out, leaving me unconscious and bleeding heavily. Fortunately, Mrs. Edmonds got the bleeding stopped, but to this day, when anyone looks down my throat they exclaim, "What happened to you?"

Despite the botched tonsillectomy, I still had a big personality and a big voice. When I moved up to Hoover High School, I became the school's head cheerleader, a big job. I also went out for basketball and baseball, but never made any waves. Someone who did make his mark in sports there was my old friend Ted Williams. Hoover High was where he began to earn the reputation that would eventually take him to the Hall of Fame.

CHAPTER FIVE

Remembering My Father

If you've got the idea that Dominic Alessio was a tough taskmaster, you'd be right. When I was still in junior high, I remember that my older brothers would go out to work every morning at seven or eight, and come home 12 hours later. Each had a little bag for their earnings and receipts, which they'd bring home to our dad. He'd count every dime and enter it into his ledger every day. On Saturdays, Dad would give both John and Louie $1.50 for their week's work.

There was another side to our father. He loved to do things with "his boys." Picnics were a favorite activity and Tijuana was a favored destination. In the early 1930s, Tijuana was still a small, undeveloped town surrounded by ranches. Crossing the line was no problem, and though prohibition was still in force in the U.S., beer was legal in Mexico.

There was a brewery in Tijuana, and we'd pick up a keg. In the photos I have, it looks like about 10 gallons. We'd find a pleasant picnic spot in the mountains, we'd eat hard cheese and salami, drink Mexican beer and have a fine time.

Prohibition stayed in force until the end of 1933, but it was legal to make and consume homemade wine. No proper Italian family would dream of sitting down to a meal without wine. Every night the Alessios had dinner together, and at the head of the table, right next to my father, was a big pitcher of our own homemade vintage. It was a special privilege for us boys, especially the younger ones, to go down into the cellar to bring up the nightly carafe.

Since, in the European tradition, we had been drinking wine almost all our lives, it was also a big temptation to sneak a couple of swigs on the sly. One weekend night, it was my turn to go down to the cellar. I had a date, and had already stashed a canning jar of wine for later. I snuck a couple of extra swallows before going upstairs to dinner.

That night, my friend Don Walstad came to pick me up in his dad's Essex. I came out clutching my jar of wine, and though it didn't taste great, we refused to throw it away. Thinking we were quite creative, we mixed it with orange pop. That tasted better, so we kept on drinking and we went to the dance feeling no pain.

Well, the upshot was, that wine did not stay down all night. Instead, I barely made it outside in time to upchuck, spaghetti and all. When the noodles started coming out my nose, Don thought I was going to die. But like the true friend he was, he stuck with me. I thought of Dad, and felt even sicker. And rightly so—not only had I stolen, I'd stolen from my own father.

Dad was a notable promoter and an astute shopper. In the early 30s, we had a Model-T and I was just learning to drive. There was a big farmers' market on 6th Street. In the early mornings between 4 and 6:30 a.m. Dad would visit with the vendors who generally had some unsold produce.

Dad was looking for bargains, and the vendors knew and liked him. He'd pay maybe fifteen cents for a crate of shopworn bell peppers. Dad and I would spend several hours and pack up the Model-T with that kind of deal, enough produce to keep our family eating for a week.

A big wholesale grocery store called Waganheimer opened next to the farmers market. One time they got stuck with fifteen or twenty cases of canned chile peppers, which customers had returned because they were too hot. They offered them to my Dad for almost nothing, so of course he snapped up this great bargain.

In those days, the Alessios were accustomed to fresh and homemade foods, rarely anything in a can. We saw those cans of peppers and thought they'd be like canned peaches or something sweet. Dessert, in other words.

When we boys decided to open up a can, what a surprise! Those chiles were so hot I thought the roof of my mouth was on fire. Louie and Frank swallowed theirs, but the rest of us almost threw up. I'm surprised the cans didn't blow up. But dessert was anything that came from a can. (You know, eventually we ate all those chiles!)

I learned many lessons from my Dad, about working hard and making friends. One lesson was really dramatic, and it happened shortly before he died.

Dad would always sit his rocking chair on our front porch, always dressed up in his vest and tie, proud of his family and his boys. Lindbergh Field had been dedicated in 1928, and a few years later, I was mowing the lawn when I noticed a small plane overhead. It started diving and weaving its way around the normal plane traffic.

This "airshow" was happening right above our house. All the neighbors were looking up at the sky, all thinking the pilot was crazy, and then it happened! He collided with another plane, and both of them crashed to earth. We could hear when they landed, about two miles away.

All of us kids started running towards the huge fire. I think Red Malloy and I were first on the scene. It was horrible; bodies lying around; blood, guts, brains. It made me kinda sick, and I had to turn around, but as I was leaving, I reached out and picked up a piece of one plane.

When I got home, Dad was on the porch. "What do you have there?" he asked.

"I don't know. I just picked it up. I wanted a souvenir," I said.

"A souvenir, huh? Do you realize how many people were killed in that crash?"

I didn't have any idea.

"Whatever the number," Dad insisted, "you don't get souvenirs from a tragedy like that!" Very quietly he got out of his chair, took the airplane part, and threw it at me. It hit me. It didn't hurt, but it hit me.

That was the maddest I ever saw my father. I felt ashamed, and I wanted to patch things up, so I went back to the crash site to search for a valuable diamond ring that had gone missing in the accident. I thought if I could find something valuable and maybe get a reward, things would be better with Dad. I never found anything, but I never forgot what he said to me, either.

It wasn't long after this, at the end of 1933, that Dad finally passed away. He was only fifty-three years old, but the West Virginia coal mines that had so aggravated his asthma caught up with him.

It was so sad that after all his hard work, he didn't live long enough to see what would finally become of his sons.

Our mother survived him by more than twenty years, and though it was a struggle, she did a great job. She got lot of help from the Edmonds, the black family that had lived next door all those years. I have always felt I've got black blood in my heart and soul, because of the Edmonds and another black family, the Cartons, who were all so good to us after Dad died.

My mother and father both gave us a wonderful heritage—a deep love of family and community. They gave us that by their example. But Dad's death left a big hole in all our lives.

CHAPTER SIX

Money, Cars and Love

Dad died in January 1933, just before my sixteenth birthday. Like my older brothers, I had been working odd jobs for years. Most of my money went to support the family, but I'd been saving my lawn mowing money, and I also made holly wreaths at Christmas, which I sold for twenty-five cents.

My older brothers all had cars, and our family car was a big Hudson. I had worked on all these cars, and made myself into a decent mechanic. It was my turn for a set of wheels. With the $60 I'd saved, I bought a run-down Model A. I set out to customize it, first with big sporty tires. Then I painted it and cut the roof down. Girls didn't mind riding in my home-made convertible.

So I had a car, but not much money, nor a regular job. And I had inherited my father's asthma. When he was alive and had bad asthma attacks, we would drive him up to Jacumba, in the mountains on the Mexican border between Tecate and Mexicali.

There were sulfur baths there, and it was quite a family resort. People from El Centro would rent houses there, and the husbands would commute. The climate and the hot springs seemed to make Dad feel better. Maybe Jacumba would help me, too.

The summer after I graduated from high school, my asthma was really bad, so I decided to try the Jacumba cure. It was sad to leave my family, but I was wheezing badly as I drove away.

By the time I crested the last hill near Jacumba, the desert heat coming up over the mountains made me feel better. Suddenly I could breathe again.

I had about $5 to my name. The Barbara Hotel had little canvas huts with wooden floors, which they rented for about $4 a week. I checked in, and knew I'd better find a job quick.

I went over to a lumber yard, where they also made ice. Two boys worked there, the owner's sons. The older one took a liking to me, and invited me to help him deliver ice. At the end of the day, he'd tell his dad, "Angelo helped me out, give him a dollar or something." Eventually, the dad gave me a steady job.

Then the family who owned the Barbara Hotel hired me to work in their amusement center in the evenings, throwing balls and giving out prizes for twenty cents an hour. Remember, this was in the heart of the Depression. I was actually able to save some money, but I missed San Diego and my family, so when I started feeling a little better, I fired up my Model A and drove back home.

Now, I'd been a flirt since grammar school, and I'd dated a little in high school. I'd been going with a sweet girl named Kathleen Gerber, a beauty who had been the "Beechnut Girl" at the county fair, but while I was gone in Jacumba she'd found someone else.

So in 1935 I was back in San Diego. I needed a job and I needed a girlfriend. I found a job at Dorman's Tire at 8th and C. I worked from eight to five in the front part of the service station pumping gas and checking oil. I got $12.50 a week, a good wage for those days.

Mr. Dorman was well liked in the community. He covered a lot of bases, with an electric shop, a repair shop, a tire shop and a grease rack. Plus, he was a U.S. Tire distributor. Because of the depression, times were tough. Mr. Dorman would sell gasoline on credit (no one had credit cards then). At the end of the month, he'd send me out with the invoices for his regular customers. I'd wear my company uniform, khakis with a little leather tie.

One of our clients was the U.S. Grant Florist, right across the street. One day I walked in with a bill, and asked for the owner, Oscar Irwin. The only person there was a girl in a smock, clipping thorns off the roses. Oscar wasn't there, she told me.

"I have an invoice here. I'll leave it with you and you'll give it to him?"

"Oh, yes," said this cute girl.

"Where did you come from?" I inquired.

"We just moved out here from Illinois," she replied. "I used to live on a farm."

"So," I remarked, "a country girl." Somehow, that didn't seem to set right with her, so I tried to smooth it over, and left with a cheery, "See you!"

Back across the street I asked my boss, "My god, who was that cute girl over there?"

"Oh, that's got to be Oscar's wife," he surmised. Now Oscar was about 35. His wife was a good looking woman, but she was Oscar's age and she limped. Certainly not my country dream girl!

The next day, I slipped across the street to say "Good morning." She looked even better, and she told me her name, Mardell. I was on my best behavior, trying to be suave enough to impress her. I made my pitch as a "good friend," but she wasn't buying it. Someone had warned her to watch out for city slickers.

I continued my routine for the next couple of weeks, each day learning a little more about her, till one day her boss caught me, and asked Mardell, "What are you wasting your time for with this Italian? If you marry him, you'll just be home having kid after kid. You know these Italians. You can do better than Angelo!"

Now, this made Mardy a little mad, but the guy was her boss and she wanted to stay on his good side. She'd also told me that, although he was married, he had from time to time made a few little moves on her, like sneaking a hug.

I didn't care what he thought, I knew Mardell liked me and I knew she was the gal I wanted. She lived on 30th Street, not far from me, and I'd offer her a ride home. When she finally accepted, I'd just drop her off in front of her house. Coming from Illinois, I guess her family thought all Italians were gangsters like Al Capone. She wouldn't invite me in.

After about a month, she told me her boyfriend Harold from Illinois was arriving the next day. But he was already too late.

"I don't like him," Mardell told her Mom, right in front of Harold.

Her mother was horrified. "He came all this way to see you, and you are not showing respect."

Harold left the next day.

And finally, I got to meet the family. I guess those Illinois winters are really chilly, because I got a freezing cold shoulder. But I had been forewarned.

"I don't know just what Mom and Dad are going to think about you," Mardy advised me, "but I want you to meet them and get it over with."

Mardy's little brother Billy was maybe four years old, and loved to play marbles, so I brought a big bagful with some of my best aggies. I got down on the floor and started playing with Billy.

Even so, the parents didn't talk to me much. I knew I'd have to impress them if Mardy and I were going to be together.

When we finally had our first "date," she warned me, "Don't just toot the horn. Come up to the door."

I got as dressed up as I could get. My brother John was quite a dandy, and I had some hand-me-downs from him. But there weren't dry cleaners around then, or at least I didn't know about them, so I used my personal pressing service—right under my mattress. I thought I looked pretty sharp.

When I got to Mardy's her parents gave me the once, twice, three-times over. I guess I passed, because they reminded me of her curfew and we were on our way out the Mission Beach Ballroom, which in the mid-30s was the hot spot on a Friday night. There were live bands, no drugs, no liquor. Well, maybe a little liquor. But all just good clean fun.

How I remember my first dance with Mardell! I didn't know if she could dance. She didn't know if I could. As it happened, I was pretty smooth, and when I took her in my arms, I realized she was great.

She looked so cute, and all my buddies came dancing by to ask, "Where did you find this one, Angelo?" Naturally, I had a smart reply. "Oh, I found her hitchhiking on the corner." Fortunately, Mardell has a sense of humor, and forgave me for that!

A good-looking basketball player from Hoover High came over and tried to pick up on Mardy. Jack Beal was a big shot at the school, but Mardy stuck with me. It was a fun night, and memorable. And that was the first night we kissed, a short, sweet kiss at her front door.

Her folks were waiting up, and Mardy told her mom, "I like Angelo. He's a nice guy and he treats me nice."

Gradually, that cold shoulder began to thaw and I started to get closer to the family. I'm sure Mardy had a lot to do with that. Eventually, I was invited for dinner.

It was a tiny house, but the greatest dinner. Mardy's mom was a wonderful cook and she made something I'd never had before: mashed potatoes and gravy. I fell in love with them that night. And then, we had—dessert! (And it wasn't hot chiles, either). I couldn't say enough complimentary things about the food, and all my comments were from the heart.

It was a Sunday night, so after dinner we all gathered around the radio and listened to Jack Benny, just like every other family in America. I could see I was making some headway.

I started taking some ribbing at work because of my romance, and I had some competition from some of the delivery guys at the U.S. Grant florists, but Mardy and I were going pretty steady and she knew how to handle herself. Everything was going fine, but I was worried about my asthma. What would happen when I had to go to Jacumba?

Eventually, I did have to go. Like before I lived a hermit's existence there, working several jobs and saving money. But I missed Mardy, and as soon as I felt well enough, I got in my little Model-A and hurried back to San Diego. Back in the 1930s the local phone exchange couldn't handle calls from far-off Jacumba, so I could only hope Mardy would be waiting for me.

I almost cry now, remembering how glad she was to see me. She made me feel great. She listened to my stories of Jacumba, and how much better I was feeling. Even Mardy's mother was glad I felt better, because she knew how much her daughter

Angelo and Mardy –
courting picture

liked me. Mardell wouldn't date anyone else, though her mom tried to convince her.

That first night I was back we went to a show downtown at the Fox Theater, one of the magnificent movie palaces of the era (it's now the Copley Symphony Hall.) Mardy looked wonderful, I felt great, and it was the loveliest evening I ever spent.

GETTING SERIOUS

We were getting serious. I developed a routine. I'd spend about five days in San Diego, and every minute of my spare time with Mardell. When I'd start choking up with asthma again, I'd have to get in my Model-A and head back to Jacumba. Mardell's reassurances helped me get through the week or so it would take me to breathe better.

Even though we spent most of the time apart, Mardy and I weren't dating anyone else. Still, I worried because of all the guys who'd come around the flower shop, and the pressure her mother put on her.

Once I showed up at her house and Mardell wasn't home. Her mother wore a pleased expression when she told me, "She went to the beach with a fella."

When I called Mardy the next day, she felt bad.

"Don't worry," she assured me. "I'll never let my mother interfere again. I won't date anyone else if you don't."

There was no question about that. We started doing little things that didn't cost much money. And I realized it was time to introduce Mardell to my mother. I was a little worried, because Mom only spoke enough English to get by. They got along fine, though; we sat around and talked and it was a fun day.

When I came back from taking Mardy home, Mom made me feel good when she said she liked "my girl" very much. She asked if I'd like to invite her for dinner.

This had never happened before. Again, I felt a little embarrassed. Mom was a great Italian cook, and I ate everything she cooked with enthusiasm, but Mardell's mother always made these great American dinners with dessert and everything.

Of course, I invited my girl, and of course she jumped at the invitation. Mom served up her classic spaghetti and meatballs. Joe and Tony were there, too, and Mardy was enjoying herself. After we finished up the pasta, something happened I'll never forget.

Mother asked, "You like-a-have-a-dessert?"

As I've said, we never had dessert.

Mom went to the kitchen and came back with a bowl of peaches. She'd gone and bought a can of peaches, to please my American girl-friend. Except for those memorable canned peppers, it was the first time we'd had dessert in the Alessio house, and Mom had done it for Mardell. And what's more, Mardy knew it. From that moment, I knew they liked each other very much.

From then on, Mardy felt comfortable coming over to my house. One time, she even came with my mother and my brother Joe to visit me in Jacumba. They brought a big spaghetti dinner, and we all dined in my little tent-cabin behind the Hotel Barbara. I'll never forget the great food and great company that night.

There were a few bumps along the path of true love. I got the mumps, and Mardy decided to ride over on her bike to visit me.

Remember our wonderful neighbors, the Edmonds, and beautiful Ellen Edmonds, my puppy love crush from first grade? Well, they still lived next door and still walked in and out of our house like family.

Imagine Mardy's surprise when she walked into my bedroom and found lovely Ellen sitting on my bed chatting, with a big jar of Vicks VapoRub that she'd brought over. I was speechless, but those two great girls got along fine, and ended up good friends.

We were really going steady now, and we developed some nice routines. I bought a nicer car, a little Plymouth coupe. Two of Mardy's cousins had good jobs as secretaries with Mobil Oil in Los Angeles. We'd visit them on Sundays, and they would show us a great time. Or we'd go to the beach or the mountains. Always, we'd come back for her mother's Sunday dinner and then listen to Jack Benny.

Now, I could put my arms around Mardy in her parents' home.

Her dad worked for the government's Work Projects Administration, the WPA, so they weren't poor. They weren't rich, but they knew how to budget. Mardell also knew how to stretch a buck; she had a great sense of style and could put together sharp looking outfits inexpensively.

By 1938, we'd been going out for almost four years, but it was still the Depression and we didn't have enough money to get married and set up housekeeping for on our own. Then, thanks to my brother Frank, I landed a really promising job.

"The first month I make $500, we'll get married," I promised Mardell.

Chapter Seven

Work and Success

My oldest brother Frank, who'd begun supporting our family when I was still a toddler back in West Virginia, had always been a hard worker. After my father died he became the head of the family.

Back in the twenties, he and Russ had started as apprentices at Hardy's Meat Market (now Young's Market) down on 5th Street. When they began, they worked inside the market but they got promoted to sales routes.

Hardy's had "semi-refrigerated" Model A Fords (don't ask me how they did that). Frank and Russ would drive house-to-house, and to small neighborhood grocery stores, where customers would wait for the "meat man" to arrive.

Frank built himself a real route; he had a great way with the housewives. He also had an ear for rhythm. He bought himself a drum and his practicing would drive us all crazy. Then he got together with a saxophone player and a banjo player. Frank wasn't much of a singer, but they made good enough music to pick up a few jobs around town.

They were known as "Frank's Californians." My favorite number was Darktown Strutters' Ball— "I'll be down to get you in a taxi, honey. Better be ready by half-past eight."

Frank was still doing his meat route, then he'd come home, change clothes and go to his gig. The Californians were in big demand; they started playing Sunday picnics. They even played some parties in Tecate. He added a piano and a trumpeter.

Then Frank got smart and opened a dance hall upstairs at Central and University. They did good business on Friday and Saturday nights.

Joe and I would take tickets at the door, and we'd clean up after the dance. Frank would slip us twenty-five cents or so.

Frank was 14 years older than me, and he married his girlfriend Gemma when I was 13 or 14. For their honeymoon they went by boat to San Francisco. They took our father with them. (It wasn't until I was a little older that I realized that was kind of unusual! Our family was always close, though.) They visited with friends and relatives in San Francisco, and when they came back to San Diego, Frank built a house around the corner from us.

Gemma had a brother back in Italy. He owned a company called Gazosa, which means carbonated, as in soda pop. He and Frank started a little bottling company in San Diego, called Gazosa Bottling.

They opened a factory on Central Avenue, but they didn't have the machines to automatically cap the bottles, so it had to be done by hand. I was still in school, and would go over with most of my other brothers to bottle and cap the cases. Gemma's brothers worked there too. Like always it was a family affair.

Those 10-ounce bottles became quite a fad around town for a while, because they had a unique sealing device. Inside the bottle was a marble, which the carbonated pop would push up to the top. To take a drink, you'd push the marble down and break the seal. When done, just shake the bottle, and the marble would "pop" back up and seal in the fizz.

The bottles were so popular, customers would hold on to them, like souvenirs. Frank had expected people to turn them in for the deposit. He began to wonder if the Italian soda business had a future. He decided to check out the local talent.

He checked out Pepsi-Cola. Pepsi was looking for a distributor, and Frank already had four trucks in operation. He signed on without paying a dime. Pepsi was associated with Rainier Beer, so Frank's new company became Pepsi-Cola Bottling and Rainier Distributors. Joe and Louie both signed on to work there.

Pepsi then came in a 12-ounce bottle, and it was wildly popular with the Indians in the back country and with Mexicans, even though at that time it had paper labels that soaked right off in the ice-water coolers. That was a problem for a while, but Pepsi always outsold Gazosa.

Frank worked hard and became one of the biggest Pepsi distributors in southern California. He was a dynamic personality. No matter where he went, people knew Frank Alessio was there. He was laughing and jolly, and everyone

The Alessio Brothers at Frank's Bottling Company (l-r) Russ, Joe, Louie, John, Tony, Angelo, Frank

loved him. He contributed to the community, especially to junior golf, and helped a lot of college students with their tuition.

He was like a second father to me. In 1938, when I was hoping to settled down with Mardy, he set me on the road to my own personal success by recommending me to George Palmer, the San Diego sales manager for International Harvester. George was looking for a new salesman, and Frank knew I was mechanically inclined.

George thought I was maybe a little too young, but he didn't settle on anyone else, so he sent me to Los Angeles to meet with Mr. Dan Keating, the District Manager.

"What makes you think you can sell trucks?" he asked me.

"Well, I can sell Pepsi-Cola and that's a hard sell," I replied.

We sat down and had a nice chat. "We'll get back to you," he said.

I drove back to San Diego, and started bugging George Palmer every chance I got. Finally he told me, "Angelo, the boss thinks you're just too young." I was about 21 at the time.

But for some reason George never did find another salesman, so he took it upon himself to hire me for $125 a month base pay plus commission. He gave me a brand new International pick-up truck to use on my route, and I could bring it home with me. That brand new half-ton pick-up sold for about $750 then. Today it would be at least $15,000.

The bad news was, he then stuck me in an office with a gigantic book to read and digest. It was the "bible" of International—all the specs for every International truck. I thought I'd go nuts. It was like being set down at a table with a 14-pound turkey and being told "Eat this!"

I plodded through and studied the specifications, and once in a while I'd sneak down to the shop and talk with the mechanics, who helped explain the different functions of a pick-up, a two-ton or a ten-ton. After three weeks, I was stir crazy.

"I've got to get out of here," I told my boss. "Let me get out and at least try selling a used truck."

Fortunately, he agreed.

SALES PITCHING

International broke San Diego up into three sales territories. Mine was Market Street south to the border. I was a little scared, but I told myself I could sell used trucks anyplace.

So I dressed up in my best suit, brought my bag of literature and set out selling in my brand-new pick-up. I made my first call at Conti Mortuary. They made headstones for the cemeteries.

Mr. Conti was Italian, and I boldly walked in to announce "I came here to see if I could help you decide on a new truck."

"A new truck? I can't even find a used one. But seeing that this is your first call, maybe I'd be interested in a used ton and a half."

Despite all my studying, I didn't know what that was. So we went out in his yard and I looked at his old truck. It had a body about 12 feet long.

"Find me something that body will fit on and we can talk," he said. He wanted a custom job, his old body with its customized work bench mounted on a newer truck chassis.

I had no idea how to find this. Back at the office, it was closing time. Another salesman had just sold a truck and taken a used Dodge ton-and-a-half in trade. I looked it over, talked to the salesman, talked to our mechanics. They all agreed it was a pretty good used truck.

The next day, I hopped in it and drove it out to 30th and Imperial. "Hey, Mr. Conti, I found you a truck."

He took a long look. "You drove it down here," he said. "How did it seem?"

"It seemed pretty good, Mr. Conti."

"Okay, I'll take it."

I could not believe this. I was beside myself with joy. I'd never sold anything so expensive. Ten cases of Pepsi sold for less than $10. I had just sold a $375 truck.

My hands shook so badly I could hardly write. Mr. Conti gave me a check, and I drove the truck back to the shop for a final tuning. My boss was in the shop with a stranger when I burst in with my $375-plus-tax check.

"Here's my first order," I blurted.

Turned out the stranger was Mr. Zimmer, in charge of sales for International for half the U.S.A. A real big shot. He was elated to have such an enthusiastic salesman on the force, and forgave my bad manners. The guys in the shop thought it was hilarious, but that was my first sale. I was now a real truck salesman.

I got a commission of $37.50 on that sale, and that's when I promised Mardy we'd get married when I made my first $500 in commissions.

"I'll think about it," I remember her saying.

"No, you're not going to think about it," I insisted.

And that was that.

Mr. Crosby

Not long after that, this cowboy brought a truck in for repairs. He told me the truck belonged to Bing Crosby, at that time one of the biggest recording and movie stars in the world. Mr. Crosby was spending most of his time in northern San Diego county at Rancho Santa Fe, but he also had a ranch in Wyoming. Once a year, he'd use this truck to haul his belongings and his three sons out to Wyoming.

"How'd you like to have a new truck?" I asked the driver. We had a sleek new one there on the floor.

"Boy, I'd love to have that one," he said longingly.

"How do you suggest we start working on that?" I inquired. He suggested we go up and see the boss.

"Who's that?" I innocently asked.

"Mr. Crosby. Bing Crosby himself. He runs the ranch."

So we went into the office. We got Mr. Crosby on the phone. I introduced myself, and told him his truck was here at International for service. Then I added I had a new truck in stock, and we could transfer his 16-foot bed. He'd have a new truck with the same bed.

Mr. Crosby didn't grasp it right away. He didn't understand how we could move the bed from one truck to the other. "Maybe we should wait till next year," he suggested.

Well, who was I to argue with Bing Crosby? I hung up, graciously, but the driver seemed disappointed.

"Maybe I should go up and talk to him in person," I offered. The driver thought that was a good idea.

The other salesmen and the mechanics had overheard my conversation, and they seemed to think it was hilarious.

"Mr. Crosby," they jibed. "Are you going to get a new truck, Mr. Crosby?"

I paid them no mind. "What time should I be there?" I asked the driver. He told me to show up at Rancho Santa Fe at 9:30 a.m., when Bing, I mean Mr. Crosby, would come back from golfing and jump in the pool with his sons.

When I got there, the boys were in the pool, and they asked me who I was, and what I was doing there.

"I'm going to sell your dad a new truck," I told them.

That got them excited—they were maybe 8 and 10 years old—and so I showed them pictures of the big red truck. They couldn't wait.

When Mr. Crosby came home the kids ran up waving the pictures and shouting, "Daddy, are we gonna buy this truck?"

"Who gave you that picture?" der Bingle asked sternly.

I stepped up to introduce myself.

"I told you on the phone we'd worry about that next year," he said ominously.

"I think I may have confused you on the phone, Mr. Crosby, " I explained. "You know, we replace truck bodies all the time." I started pitching a two-speed rear axle, and how it would help him, especially on his long drive to Wyoming.

Now, the old truck was still in the shop. I didn't know what, if anything was wrong with it. But it was in for repairs.

Mr. Crosby calls his foreman. He comes over and states that the old truck is in pretty good shape, but Mr. Crosby insists he listen to me. Mr. Crosby himself listens when I promise we can have his new truck ready and delivered before he leaves for Wyoming next week.

Finally, he says, "Let me tell you, you little Italian. If I buy this truck and it doesn't do what you say it's going to do, I'm going to run you right down Broadway and you're going to jump in the bay."

I thought that might be great advertising. I can just see the headlines: "Bing Crosby Chases Angelo Alessio Down Broadway. Alessio Jumps in Bay."

"Okay," I tell him. "It's a deal."

He asks me about a trade-in for his old truck. Then Mr. Crosby tells me to write it up. I'm flabbergasted. This time, too, my hands are shaking. He autographs the purchase order. Signed, sealed, and delivered next week.

I get back to the office around noon. The mechanics are outside, eating lunch.

"Oh HI, Mr. Crosby," they call. "How are you today? How was the golf?"

They give me a hard time for maybe 15 minutes before I ask them, "Gentlemen, are you all done?"

They laugh harder. "Yes, Mr. Crosby, we're all done."

"Gentlemen," I say, barely able to contain myself. "Would you look at this order and tell me what name is on it?"

I pass the order down, and all is silent. Those smart-mouthed mechanics are all speechless.

Now, I'd taken Mr. Crosby's old truck in trade, and I didn't even know what was wrong with it. I asked the mechanic in charge—they had only had to replace a single spark plug. I thought to myself, "If he ever finds that out he'll chase me into the bay for sure!"

When the driver came to pick up the new, hybrid truck the next week, he was delighted. He thanked me over and over. I was still a little worried, but the new truck worked perfectly. There was never a problem, and from that time on, any time his family needed new trucks, Mr. Crosby would say, "Call the little Italian."

THE REAL PAYOFF

As you can see, I was having some success as a truck salesman. I didn't forget my promise to Mardell, and after maybe nine months, a year at International, I picked up a check for $565.

I raced over to Mardy's and announced, "Get ready. We're going to get married!"

Her mother still had her objections. "You can't afford it," she protested.

"I can afford it, " I insisted. "I've got a good job, I'm going to be a good salesman, and I'm going to make good money. And we're going to get married!"

I guess I sold her, and Mardy was already sold. We had a simple wedding. Mardy made her own darling outfit. My eldest brother Frank was best man and he threw a little breakfast party. The bridesmaids were Mardy's two cousins from L.A.

We were married in the little chapel in Balboa Park on May 1, 1940, by a priest the park supplied. It was not a Catholic wedding. Mardy wasn't Catholic, and I was not very observant. I wouldn't say we were very religious, but we were taught to do the right thing. My father taught us to be good to everyone, and Mom felt the same. Most important, Mom liked Mardy, and was happy with the wedding.

We borrowed a new car from Russ Romano, a family friend, and drove to Palm Springs for a few days. Then we went over to Catalina. That was our honeymoon.

We came home and looked for a place to live. We found a nice duplex cottage at Copeland and El Cajon Boulevard, not too far from my mom. The landlord lived nearby and kept the place immaculate. It was small, maybe 1000 square feet, but comfortable. To me it seemed really luxurious, because of the crowded conditions I'd grown up with. Here it was just Mardy and me, with our own bathroom, kitchen, living room and bedroom, and all for just $55 a month.

When Mardy's parents saw how happy we were, they warmed up to me. From the first, Mardy was a great little wife, and a talented cook. In about a year, our first child Rosalie was born.

Part II

Hard Work Bears Fruit

CHAPTER EIGHT

The Mexico Connection

John was born the middle child of the seven Alessio brothers. He was only 10 when we moved to San Diego, with only a fifth grade education, but Dad put him to work at a downtown shoeshine stand to help support the family.

When we were all kids, Johnny didn't particularly stand out, but he always had a way with people, and could make you feel good about yourself. With his brothers, he focused on working together. What was special was John's vision. He could always see the big picture. He looked ahead, saw what was on the horizon, and then well beyond that.

We Alessios were hard working and ambitious, and by the 1940s we were all doing well in our own endeavors, working together and helping each other out when we could. It took John Alessio and his vision to open doors we never dreamed existed. To this day, I can hardly believe where those doors led us.

Starting in the 1920s, when the Alessios first arrived in San Diego, John worked at the shoeshine stand at 5th and E, near the Bank of America. One of his regular customers was a public relations man for the Bank, C. Arnholt Smith. Tall, well dressed, he was a real man-about-town.

Every so often, John would suggest to Mr. Smith, "Please give me a job at the bank."

Mr. Smith would try to be kind and let him down easy. After all, John was a grammar school dropout. A lowly shoeshine boy. "You don't have any experience, John. What could you do at the bank?"

Years passed. Mr. Smith rounded up some financing and opened the U.S. National Bank at 2nd and Broadway. His brother, an oil man from Texas, helped him get going, and the bank took off right away.

Mr. Smith still kept getting his shoeshines from John, and John kept asking for a job.

For years, Mr. Smith had a professional relationship with a Tijuana bank, Banco del Pacifico, so when he became CEO of U.S. National, he associated with them as a correspondence bank for international transactions. In this era, many Italian immigrants were living in Tijuana, while they waited for their U.S. Visas to come through.

Many of these Italians opened businesses and restaurants in Tijuana, and did business with Banco del Pacifico. And many of them spoke only Italian—neither English nor Spanish. Someone at the bank complained to Mr. Smith, "We need to find a translator."

Mr. Smith summoned John to the bank. "Here's the break you've been waiting for. It won't pay much, but if you want to try it, I'll recommend you."

John would have paid them for the experience.

"Go down and work for a year, " Mr. Smith said. "Then come see me. By then you'll have banking experience and we'll be able to use you."

C. Arnholt Smith was already on his way to becoming a legend in San Diego. Throughout his career, he was to many a controversial figure, but he was always a loyal friend to the Alessio family. Getting Johnny the job at Banco del Pacifico was the first big favor he did for us, but it was far from the last. From now on, in this narration, I'll refer to him as "Arnie."

⁂

Johnny was still living at home when he started commuting to Tijuana in the $200 car he'd bought with his shoeshine money. He was making about $250 a month, not too bad in those Depression days.

He did translations for the bank, and pretty soon the Italian clients would speak only to him. One Italian in Tecate had a vineyard of about 100 acres. He worshipped John, and wouldn't do any business without consulting him first. He changed his will, and left the whole vineyard to Johnny.

Like all of us, Johnny was a hard worker, but he took it to extremes. He did nothing but work. He ate, slept, dreamt Banco del Pacifico. He had no hobbies but doing a good job for the bank's clients. The Mexicans picked up on that, too, and many asked Johnny to affiliate with them as a partner in their various businesses.

One of these new partners was Angelo Serena, who owned Serena Restaurant and Bar in Tijuana. When we entered World War II after the Japanese bombed Pearl Harbor in 1941, there was all sorts of rationing in the U.S., from gasoline to rubber to food. Those days you couldn't get real butter or a good steak in the U.S, so people would cross over to Mexico for a real meal. Angelo put out an unbelievable dinner: big juicy steak and all the butter you could eat. The place stayed packed, and Johnny made a bundle.

That was just one business. Johnny made many more deals: lumber yards, the paint business, more restaurants. The more successful Johnny became, the more generous he was. He had a real weakness for kids and orphanages, and supported charitable institutions on both sides of the border. And he never forgot his family. His brothers were often included in his deals, and he never had a loser.

Johnny was already at Banco del Pacifico when I graduated from Hoover High in 1934, and Johnny had a proposition for me. He had noticed that a lot of Indians, or as they're now called, Native Americans, living in the mountains and deserts of Northern Mexico would gather gold pebbles on their lands, and bring them into the bank. For about $15 a trip, I'd pick up the little bags of raw gold and bring them up to San Diego for appraisal. The assayer would melt it into bars, which I'd bring back to Johnny's bank. I did this for a year or so. (I'd show the gold bars to my friends and say, "Look at this bar. Now, that's a Hershey!")

With no training and a fifth-grade education, Johnny began working his way up in the international banking business. They loved him at Banco del Pacifico; little did he know that one of the owners was the President of Mexico. This would soon prove advantageous to the Alessio brothers.

CRACKS

Frank, our oldest brother, had gotten me my job at International Harvester, but Johnny helped me out there, too. My sales territory went down to the Mexican border, but back then, financing a truck in Mexico was just about impossible, so no one even tried to sell there. But Johnny was moving up in the ranks at Banco del Pacifico, and when one of the officers wanted to help out a friend, my brother called me.

Mr. Mesa wanted to talk about a truck. He was a big lumber man in Baja. Now, there's not a lot of wood in Baja California, so most of it is imported. Mr. Mesa brought wood down from Los Angeles for resale.

Mr. Mesa needed a big truck. I was still new on the sales force, and I knew my way around a pick-up or a ton-and-a-half. I talked to the mechanics, of course, and I also went out of my way to ask questions from truckers when they brought their vehicles in for repair. What components did they like? What problems did they have? That big old "bible" I'd reluctantly studied had many of the details, but there is nothing like information from the person who drives the truck.

When you buy a truck, it's not like going to a car dealer, choosing a model and picking out your options. For a two-ton or larger truck, you analyze each component: engine, transmission, differential, auxiliary transmission, wheels, brakes, tires, then basically build a custom vehicle.

Mr. Mesa needed at least a five-ton truck. He'd be towing a 30-foot trailer, and he'd need to haul 10 to 15 tons of wood. I didn't have a computer. I had to fill out a paper form, figure the price, add the tax, and add it all up. I was nervous.

I specified the biggest engine International had, a 450-cubic inch, heavy duty motor; an F52 transmission. Everything added up to a little more than $8000, but I wrote in a discount, and Mr. Mesa gave me a check.

"Make sure you tell Johnny I gave you this check," he said, because Johnny was financing the sale.

I was so excited, I rushed into the sales office, waving the check at my manager.

He looked at my paperwork, and didn't say anything for a minute. It was our first Mexican sale, and we weren't even taking a trade in, and he liked that a lot. Then he started laughing, and he couldn't seem to stop.

"You did a great job," he finally choked out. "Everything's fine except for one little thing: they're going to have to drive their new truck on roller skates."

Yes, I had completely forgotten the wheels and tires. I wanted to die. Fortunately, we still had a little profit built into the deal. My boss didn't want to blow it, so we included the tires and ate the cost. "I want this order down there in Mexico," he said, "and you sold him the right truck."

It was the first new truck imported into Tijuana for as long as anyone could remember. When the driver came to pick it up, he told me, "Angelo, this thing goes uphill with a big load like it's nothing."

Even though I'd made a dumb mistake, this turned out to be a smart deal in the long run. Word got around Baja California that if you needed a truck, go see Johnny's little brother Angelo. Soon I was selling to every lumber yard and liquor distributor down there.

I connected, too, with the Aldrette family, the biggest wheat growers in Baja. Mr. Aldrette was influential politically, and he ended up owning the Tecate Brewery. They needed many, many trucks, and I sold them all. I always say, I had Mexico in my back pocket, because anyone in northern Baja California who wanted to buy a truck came to Angelo Alessio. Not only did I have a reputation for selling the correct truck to each customer, but, thanks to Johnny, my clients could get financing in Mexico.

Not all of my Mexican deals worked out so smoothly. Once, during World War II, Johnny asked me to meet with a General Gonzales in Ensenada. Because of the war, U.S. truck production was greatly reduced, but I went down to see what I could do.

Neither General Gonzales nor his aide spoke much English. My Spanish was not too good. It took us a couple of hours, but they had some pictures of what they wanted: transportation to haul Mexican soldiers. Two-ton trucks with flatbeds.

After much laborious discussion, I signed the General up for twelve trucks, a very big deal. He signed all my forms and told me he'd bring a purchase order to San Diego the next week. The General and all his entourage walked into the shop, to the amazement of all the guys.

I introduced my prestigious client to my boss, and we all went out to dinner, the margaritas flowing like water. Then we went bar hopping. By then, the General and I were buddy-buddy: at one point, he hugged me. In public. You don't often see a Mexican general hugging an Italian/American truck salesman. I was surprised, to say the least, and my buddies didn't let me hear the end of it, either.

That day, I must have spent about $250. Believe me, that was a lot of money in those days. Then, we waited. Time went by, and the trucks weren't delivered. It took a year to finally realize that the first fleet of trucks I had sold would never reach the customer. The U.S. government needed every truck for the war effort. In the end, we couldn't deliver even a single one of the dozen trucks General Gonzales had ordered. Fortunately, the Mexican military didn't blame me.

Around this time, Dan Keating, that guy in L.A. who hadn't wanted to hire me, had a bright idea to start the "Triple Diamond Club." International used a triple diamond on their logo, and the club was to recognize the best salesmen. I always came up second or third, and soon all the heavy hitters in Los Angeles knew who Angelo Alessio was.

⚜

By 1945, I was doing well at International, but the honchos felt they weren't doing enough business in East San Diego, from Euclid Avenue towards La Mesa. They wanted to add a dealership out there, and asked me if I'd like to open one.

I was surprised. What did I know about running a dealership? Plus, I had developed some great, loyal accounts. They were like insurance policies that kept paying off year after year. I agreed to open a dealership in East San Diego if I could keep my big accounts. That was good for the company, too, so they agreed.

Now today, if you wanted to open a dealership, it would cost you $250,000-plus. I was honest with the company: I had about $700 saved up in my personal bank account.

The war was still going on. I figured I could scrape up about $2,000. Guess what. Dan Keating came back to me and told me to go ahead.

In those days, International would finance your new truck inventory. They would "floor" you at almost zero percent interest. They'd supply you with your parts inventory and payment would be due in 90 days. They'd even let you extend that for two more 90-day periods. I knew I could get new parts and trucks. I went up to Los Angeles and scrounged around for used parts and tools.

I was ready to go, but I needed a location. I found an old garage at 47th and El Cajon Boulevard. The owner, I think his name was Webster, was doing auto repairs there. I explained to him that I'd need mechanics for my new dealership. I offered to pay them by the hour, and he could keep the service charges. I'd furnish parts at cost, and help finance the work, in turn for rent on the place. Mr. Webster agreed.

We shook hands on the deal: things were different then. A few days later I put up the biggest sign of my life: "Alessio Motor Sales International Harvester Truck Dealer."

What an exciting day that was. Being my own boss at my own dealership meant working even harder. I made all the sales. I wrote up all the job tickets, I did my own bookkeeping. I even delivered all the invoices. It was 18 hour days as a rule.

The first Alessio Motors location – July 1, 1945

I had to watch out for trade-ins. Every time I took one, I'd bought a truck. Bank of America agreed to tide me over with those small loans when I didn't have the cash. And my strategy was, when things were going well, I'd borrow, say, $5,000, put it in a safe deposit box, pay the interest for a few months, then pay the whole note off. After a few times, my credit was good.

In just over a year, when I saw that this new venture was working out, I bought out Mr. Webster for about $2500.

By this time, our first son Larry was born. Mardy and I found a house in a nice area on 58th Street. For just $5,000, we had a home of our own.

CHAPTER NINE

Off to the Races

In 1947, Johnny, the former shoeshine boy, was President of Banco del Pacifico, which was then bankrolling the weekend operations of Tijuana's Agua Caliente racetrack. Opened in 1928, Caliente was running horse races on Saturdays and Sundays. It was one of Tijuana's largest employers, with about 600 workers, plus they needed cash on hand to pay off winning bets.

The track operator, Augie Silvera, would borrow about half a million dollars every weekend. On Monday, he was to return the $500K plus interest and a handling charge. After a while, though, Caliente stopped paying the interest and charges. Sometimes they'd even bring back less than the original loan.

Finally, Johnny told Augie he'd best look for another bank. "I can't explain these shortages anymore."

Augie panicked. None of the other banks would lend him anything either.

The next day, Johnny got a call from Mexican President Miguel Alemán Valdes. Because he was an investor in Banco del Pacifico, Johnny had already made his acquaintance. El Presidente was worried about losing all those local jobs if the racetrack closed. He wanted to know what the problem was.

"Señor Alemán, they're not bringing back all our money," Johnny explained.

"Well, I want to try it a little longer," the president said. "But I want you to go out there, Johnny. Take a look around and see why they're not bringing back the bank's money."

Johnny didn't want to get involved in the racetrack. He knew little about the track or its operations. But since the President of Mexico had personally asked him, what could he do?

He began showing up on the weekends, taking detailed notes. It didn't take long to turn up some problems. First, Mr. Silvera had horses of his own, and was making his own bets instead of watching the business. The kitchen wasn't doing much business: they bought food, but most of it disappeared out the back door. There was another leak in the barns: most of the hay the track provided to feed the horses also disappeared, and the owners didn't pay.

Though Johnny confronted Augie, the situation didn't improve. The President asked Johnny to consider running the racetrack and the bank. My brother didn't want any part of it.

The situation continued to deteriorate until the racetrack owed the bank almost $800,000. The President and the other investors in Banco del Pacifico kept pressuring Johnny to take over and run the racetrack.

Our middle brother called a meeting of all the Alessio brothers. He had told the bank investors he would need his brothers' help to plug the holes plaguing Caliente, and that they would all need the required work permits.

By this time, Russ, the second oldest, owned a bar at 4th and F in downtown San Diego. It was still a kind of rough part of town, with a lot of sailor business. He had started doing a little bookmaking on the side, not exactly legal, but he had developed a friendly relationship with the local cops by feeding the homeless and keeping the neighborhood peaceful. So they seemed to overlook his extra-curricular activities.

The bookmaking was informal, and small scale, but Russ knew how to figure a horse, so he made a little profit on it.

When Johnny called the brothers together, we met at Russ's bar. We were all doing well on our own, but we all wanted to help out. Frank couldn't, because his thriving Pepsi bottling and distributing business demanded all of his time.

Russ and little brother Tony would run the "foreign book," the backbone of the business. It should turn in at least a 20 percent profit.

Joe would run the photo finish. Louie, our quiet brother who never married, had enjoyed cooking in the Army during the war. He would take over the kitchen: Saturdays and Sundays could be big business days for a restaurant at the track.

Johnny, of course, would be General Manager. He would deal with the unions, and handle all the politics, a full-time job in Mexico. Lucky for us, he was already a master politician.

With my mechanical ability and background, I was to be in charge of "facilities management": the upkeep and maintenance of the physical plant. That would include running the barn, keeping the water system working, and maintaining the track itself. The water demands were unbelievable because we kept that turf irrigated 24 hours a day; sometimes we needed as many as 26,000 gallons a day.

Looking for a permanent water source, I drilled some holes on the racetrack grounds, but they were dry. Right down the hill was the old Agua Caliente Hotel, which had been popular with the Hollywood crowd until the Mexican government outlawed gambling. The grand old hotel was now a school. As you might guess from the name "Hot Water," the hotel had also been a spa. There was a permanent water supply there, but the wells would need to be rebuilt, a big, expensive job.

So I made a deal with the city and the state of Baja California that we would supply the school with water, if we could have two or three wells of our own. I built a million-gallon reservoir tank at the track. Keeping the construction job running smoothly was hard enough. Trying to keep people from stealing our water made it worse.

Eventually, we ended up supplying many, many schools and quite a few nearby homes with water. Our pipeline ran through the old Agua Caliente golf course, and for a while they too were stealing our water. But we did have a reliable water source, and without it we would have had to close the track.

Yet another problem presented itself. Customers were supposed to pay $2 at the front gate, but many would just pay what they could. I brought down my father-in-law to straighten that out.

Bookkeeping isn't the most exciting part of doing business, but it has to be done right. Racetrack bookkeeping is a specialty, and requires a sharp CPA, but at Caliente, the accounting was a real mess when we took over. It seems that no one had actively managed the track for more than a few years. Americans would go down, do pretty well, then think, "Hey, we're dealing with Mexicans, let's play our own little game."

Mexican laws are different, but people are the same way everywhere. Mexicans are smart, and they are proud. Previous American operators had been caught stealing from the government, cheating on their taxes, and they got run out of Mexico. Now that we Alessios had committed to this project, we made sure that wouldn't happen to us.

Unions are a strong presence in Mexico, and they became even stronger after we took over Caliente and the employees began earning more. The Sindicato Rojo, the Red Union, was in charge of the track workers. But though our employees were well compensated, their paychecks seemed rarely to make it home to their families. The workers would stop after work and play dominoes, an obsession in Tijuana.

A committee of wives came to Caliente and begged Johnny, "Please do something so we can have money enough to run our families."

Somehow, Johnny worked it out with the pay cashiers that the wives could come in and draw against their husbands' salaries. It worked out. And as tough as the union was, we got along with them better than I ever would have expected.

⚜

A year or so later, Caliente was doing well. We had paid off the old bank loan, cleared the other debts, and had a $400,000 reserve. We Alessios had our hands full, but it felt good. We were a family working together.

We were, however, foreigners working in Mexico. We wanted to solidify our position, but as American citizens we could not legally own a business in Mexico. We made a deal with the racetrack owners; they redistributed some of their shares. We were investing our hard work, and producing good results, but for the whole time we were running Caliente there was never a written contract. The owners of the racetrack were an S.A.: Sociedad Anonima. A corporation. From time to time, people would arrive and announce themselves as investors. We never knew. The corporation was an "anonymous society."

We Alessios always felt accepted by our Mexican associates. We worked on a handshake. We trusted them and they always knew it, and they trusted us as well.

Eventually Johnny gave up his position at Banco del Pacifico. He had many financial interests in Mexico, by now he spoke fluent Spanish, and he always made sure we hired Mexican attorneys for Caliente. We always complied with all the Mexican laws, including work permits for foreign citizens we employed there. We also complied with the local customs. For instance, all the betting was done in American dollars, because the peso just went up and down.

Of course, we also dealt with la mordida. Literally it means "little bite," but in practice it means a bribe, and it's how you got things done in Mexico, at least when we were doing business there. For us, we called it "a friendly handshake, " and when you were shaking the hand, you'd have a $50 bill in yours. That was a small mordida then; if you needed a larger favor from a government official, la mordida might fill a good-sized envelope.

To the Dogs

The track was running smoothly. A few years later, we found a way to make it even more profitable. In 1953 the Alessio brothers got to know the Funk brothers. They had a greyhound dog track in Phoenix. Dog racing was legal in Arizona, and they were doing well there. They wanted to try greyhound racing in Tijuana.

We had to get the permit; they were to pay for the improvements to run a dog track. We would share profits, if any, at the end of the year. We checked out the Funk family. They were in the jewelry business, had a clean reputation, knew their business. We welcomed them.

They helped the business at Caliente. Dogs ran every day of the year, and the dog bettor is a different customer. And to our surprise, the Mexican bettors loved the dogs.

It is much cheaper overall to run dogs than horses. Horsemen need barns and hay,

Greyhound winner in Arizona: (center l-r) Senator Giss (owner of winning dog), actress Debra Padget, Angelo

and that's expensive. Horse owners also expect the track to put up a purse of $1500 to $10,000, depending on the class of horse.

In contrast a dog owner would have at least 20 dogs. Kennels were smaller than stables, and we weren't responsible for feeding the dogs. The racetrack didn't pay a purse—the winner of each race got a percentage of the money bet, and so did the second, third and fourth-place dogs. The track had no expense there.

With dog racing the biggest cost was lighting the track at night, and we could handle that. When the Funk brothers invited the Alessios to move into the Arizona dog circuit, I checked it out, but we decided to wait. Interesting things were happening in the horse racing world.

Johnny had invented something that was the first of its kind in the horse racing world. It was copied eventually by all the other tracks. It was a "book" called the "5-10," which meant the bettor picked the winning horses from the fifth race through the tenth.

It was like today's Lotto. The person who picked all of the winners won the pool, which sometimes got to be as much as $85,000 to $100,000 for a single, two dollar bet.

People throughout southern California formed 5-10 Clubs, and assigned one person to come down to Tijuana to place their bet. It became a fad. At the end of each racing day, we'd announce the winner. Everyone was checking their bets, but if there wasn't a winner, the pool would parlay to the next 5-10. Sometimes it got up to $250,000.

In those days that was a fortune. The winners would always insist on taking their winnings in cash. We didn't want them going out on the streets with that much money; we always gave them an overseer, to make sure they'd make it back safely to the U.S. That saved problems, and we got good publicity in the papers.

❧

We got a lot of publicity then, partly because movie stars enjoyed coming down from L.A. to bet on the horses. We established a VIP room at Caliente, and once every three or four weeks I'd go down for the weekend to be the host.

Our staff would tell me, "Your surprise today will be Victor Mature." Or George Raft. Or Ben Gazarra. Or Liz Taylor.

Liz would come down with her newest husband, Eddie Fisher. We fed them margaritas, which she especially loved. She was such a beautiful girl, and it was shocking how much my wife Mardy looked like her! To me, of course, Mardy always had more inner depth and beauty, but Liz and I did always get along really well.

One day I remember vividly. Liz was well relaxed with margaritas, and decided she wanted to go shopping in downtown Tijuana. She had it in mind to buy a particular fabric that she'd heard was a good buy there. My heart skipped a beat. She and Eddie were a huge Hollywood scandal, then, and I couldn't imagine how we could keep them safe in downtown Tijuana.

I couldn't talk her out of it, though. I borrowed Johnny's right-hand man, Freddie, to drive us downtown. He escorted us in my Cadillac, with Liz in the front seat.

Freddie had called ahead, found the right shop, and arranged for a policeman to reserve us a parking spot. Liz and Eddie were, of course, immediately recognized. Soon, we could barely move. Liz was hard to please. She looked at many rolls of fabric before she made her decision.

We made it back to my car and went back to watch a couple more dog races. Liz was a heavy smoker, and she filled up all the ashtrays in my Caddy. After the races, she didn't want to fight the line at the border, which at the time might have been maybe an hour long.

I volunteered to drive Liz and Eddie across the border in their own car. We got a special police escort, sirens and all. It wasn't that uncommon for us to do this for our VIP visitors, but the Fishers felt like royalty, and when we got them across the border in no time, they couldn't believe it.

I jumped out of the car and said, "There you are. Have a good time!" They were so happy they invited me and Mardy to be their guests in Vegas, where Eddie Fisher was a big star.

This kind of publicity wasn't unusual for Caliente in those days. It did seem like Hollywood loved the Alessio brothers.

In our family, though, things were a little more basic. When I got back home from this particular weekend, my kids were enchanted.

Rosalie was a huge fan of Elizabeth Taylor. When I mentioned that I had an ashtray full of Liz's cigarette butts, she was thrilled. She planned to put them all in bag and take them to school. My sons Larry and Steve planned to make some money on them. Everyone in school wanted Liz Taylor's cigarette butts.

CHAPTER TEN

Harvesting the Fruit of Hard Work

It was 1951. San Diego had grown to more than 333,000; Robert O. Peterson opened his first Jack-in-the-Box drive-through at 63rd and El Cajon Boulevard, only blocks from my International dealership. That was the year my CPA attached a short note to my financial statement. "Congratulations," it said. "You are now a millionaire."

I was surprised, but I didn't change anything I was doing. I just went to work the next day and thought about making another million.

I had known I was moving forward, and my truck dealership showed a profit every month. What I hadn't realized was that all the little rental properties I had picked up along the way, and the extra money from the race track really added up.

It really just boiled down to one four-letter word: w-o-r-k. Work, work, work. I knew that if I put in the work, it would pay off. We Alessios were brought up to work from the time we were kids, and of the seven brothers, I'd say five did really well. Four of us, John, Frank, Russ and I, did super well.

The original International Harvester dealership was still operating on Main Street in San Diego, but my East San Diego outlet on El Cajon Boulevard was doing much more business. I had cornered most of the

Alessio Motors – the distributorship

parts business and truck sales, so the corporation suggested we cease competing with ourselves. They offered me an exclusive dealership for all of San Diego and Imperial Counties if I would put up a suitable building.

I found a property at Euclid and Federal adjoining Highway 94. It was about five and three-quarter acres, and I especially liked it because of the location. On a map, if you put a pin in it, it was about the same distance from Tijuana, downtown San Diego, El Cajon and Mission Valley. Reps from International came out and gave it their blessing, so I dickered with the owner, Mr. Goodman, and got the price down from $300,000 to $200,000.

I talked to our old family friend, Arnie Smith, then the acknowledged "Mr. San Diego." I borrowed from his U.S. National Bank to buy the property and for another $250,000 built a beautiful 35,000 square foot building with a large service department. I'll give you some free advice here: that's the secret to a successful truck dealership: a large, modern service department with strong parts and sales departments.

So I now had one of the finest truck dealerships in southern California, and some of the biggest accounts: R.E. Fenton, Western Metal, and Quality Dairy, to mention just a few.

My daughter Rosalie was already married, and I hired my son-in-law as sales manager. We had about 10 salesmen altogether. I still did a lot of the "heavy stuff"—selling the big trucks—and we did very well there.

Angelo as pictured in Automotive News, 6/3/68

We were doing so well that eventually we attracted some competition. Kenworth Trucks came from Seattle to explore the possibilities, but even when they opened a dealership, I continued to do well.

Next, White Motors came along and decided this was fertile territory. So now there's a real competition going in San Diego.

General Motors made a stab, but I knocked them out of the box. Peterbilt, a very good truck maker, moved in with their specialty, dump trucks. Still, after a 25-year association with International, my business continued to thrive.

A district manger from White Motor in Portland asked if I wanted to sell. The idea had never crossed my mind, but I visited him and he was very interested. We didn't immediately come together on a price, but we were getting close. I felt obligated to International to let them know. I told them I wanted to get out.

They weren't thrilled with the idea. We'd been in San Diego County for so many years, and done a good business. We had many loyal customers.

"We're not going to let some White dealer come in and take our location and use our reputation to break into San Diego. We've been there too long," the execs told me.

We had been together a long time. "Okay," I told them. "I own the property the dealership sits on, and I don't want to sell the land, but I will sell you just the business."

They thought it over, and eventually we made a deal. I got a 20-year lease from International, an excellent return on my investment. They paid me for my parts inventory, more than a quarter million dollars, and another $100,000 for my equipment. I owed nothing on any of it.

International brought in a long-time employee and financed him to act as their dealer. He knew the business, but came in with very little money. That was fine with me; International had guaranteed the deal. It was time to move on. There was no shortage of other things to do.

BACK ON TRACK

Caliente was still hot. Johnny was running the show and the whole operation was turning a profit. Fresh ideas kept coming along on how we could increase business. I don't recall who had the original thought, but someone came up with this new winner.

First, a little background for those unfamiliar with race tracks and betting. The "foreign book" at Caliente was nothing more than betting on races at other tracks. You've probably heard it described as book betting, but we called it "foreign book." Individuals would come in and bet against the book, in this case, the Alessios.

Here's how it worked. Everyone's heard of the great Kentucky Derby, held at Churchill Downs every May. Around January, brother Tony would start to study all the horses nominated to run in the Derby.

At that time, at least 100 horses would be named, but as months passed things would change, depending on which races the horses ran, which they won, what horses they had run against, how much weight they had carried, and many other factors. All these things would affect the odds.

Tony was horse savvy. He would find every book he could find and study all the horses and their charts. He'd make his own odds to put on our board. Early in the process, any horse he considered a possible runner he'd give odds of 50 or 100 to one. Horses he thought

John at Caliente as pictured in The Saturday Evening Post *(Nov. 15, 1958)*

unlikely to make it into the Derby he'd offer at 1,000 to one. You wouldn't believe how many people will bet on a horse just because they think, "How can we not take these odds?"

As weeks went by, Tony would drop those long odds to 800 or 700, as it became clear they might actually run the race. At the same time, some horses had already dropped out—most of those had started at 200 or 1000 to one odds, which covered us well. Now the money that people had paid in on those real long shots was securely in the kitty, building up the Derby pool. As race day got nearer, Tony would drop the odds to 20 or 15 to one.

It was an exciting time. The board would be posted at Caliente with all the horses and their odds. People would see a horse at 100 to one and think, "Gotta take that bet."

Of course, a real horse player is almost like someone playing the stock market. They study the horses, know them like family, how far they've run, how much weight they carry, all those other variables.

One time I decided to play a joke on everyone. I got one of the oldest nags around, and I dressed up like a Kentucky Colonel. I brought the horse onto the field, and bragged about it over the loudspeaker. That pitiful creature probably couldn't even run five minutes, let alone win the Derby. It was quite a show. It took a few minutes, but finally people started getting the joke, and everyone had a good laugh.

Tony, meanwhile, was doing his job, protecting Caliente from all that wild betting. He knew what he was doing, and he did it by actually living the Derby.

A few days before the race, he'd go to Kentucky. By race day, Caliente's pool would be $75,000 or $150,000 on that single race. One year I went with him and saw how he took care of things.

By then, Tony had been doing this for 10 or 15 years. He got a lot of recognition there. Everybody knew him. He'd watch how people were betting, write down each price change, and if he felt things weren't going right, he'd use money from the Caliente betting pool to cover our bets. That way, he'd make sure we didn't take too severe a hit.

The Kentucky Derby was Tony's day to shine. His name was on the lips of smart bettors across the country and around the world. His name was in the paper, sometimes, even his picture. Little did we know then what all this great publicity could bring.

CHAPTER ELEVEN

Mama Said, Mama Said

U nlike our Dad, who died while three of his sons were still teenagers, our mother lived to see all the brothers grown and doing well. Even after we were married and fathers, and even grandfathers, she referred to us as "my boys." And though she had suffered much and survived it all, she was always a worrier. Well, she was a MOM.

Once we started having children of our own, she'd always warn us, "Watcha the baby, watcha the baby. Kidnap, kidnap!" Maybe it was her upbringing in the wilds of southern Italy; maybe it was our unexpected financial success. She especially pounded this into her daughters-in-law, our wives.

*(l-r) rear: John, Louie, Russ, Frank, Joe
front: Tony, Rose, Angelo*

Whenever she started on this theme, we'd wait until she wasn't looking, exchange smiles and shake our heads. Who would want to kidnap our kids, we told ourselves. We were just seven Italian boys from West Virginia, trying to live out the American dream. Nobody special here!

Mom died in 1955. Needless to say, Mother's warnings were long forgotten by 1960.

By then, San Diego's population was almost 600,000. The county had more than a million inhabitants. This was no longer a quiet

California backwater: this was a major metropolis. And the Alessio family name was well known, not just in San Diego but through-out the south-western United States and northern Mexico. Our name was often in the papers, frequently for our charitable con-tributions in Tijuana— helping people with businesses, schools, hospitals, road repairs, underground water piping.

One of the Alessio school openings: (l-r front) Rubin Bejarano, a Governor of Baja, Mardy, Angelo, John

All the action at Caliente brought increasing publicity to the Alessio brothers. The coming of the greyhounds, the endless parade of Hollywood stars, the new betting gimmicks we dreamed up; all con-tributed to our local and national notoriety.

We'd earned a reputation among the rich and famous that we'd take almost any bet, for any amount. That practically guaranteed front-page coverage, especially when someone hit it big.

And finally, Tony and his "foreign book" were bringing throngs of new customers and fame to Caliente. There were stories in local and national magazines about him and Johnny, and sometimes photographs. The track was on the list of must-see destinations for tourists in south-ern California. And everyone wanted to meet Johnny or Tony.

Since Tony was my only "little brother," the one I had looked out for all our lives, we were especially close, and I was especially proud of his accomplishments. He had become so expert at handicapping high profile races, especially the Kentucky Derby, that he had a worldwide reputation for his knowledge of the horses, trainers, jockeys and tracks. People called from all over to ask his advice. The year I went with him to the Derby, they just wouldn't leave him alone. All the big-wigs came up and wanted to shake his hand. I was so proud of him, it was like he was my own kid.

Maybe because he was the youngest in our big, rowdy family, Tony had always liked things neat and clean. He and his wife Virginia had bought a lovely home in a quiet part of town just east of San Diego State University. In Alvarado Estates, everyone had an acre of land, high hedges, gardens, swimming pools and built-in privacy.

They lived there with their young daughters Toni and Denise, and a live-in maid. They had two white Cadillacs: a sedan and a convertible. It was a neat, orderly life, just the way Tony liked things. Most mornings, he left the house just after 8 a.m. in the hardtop Cadillac. He'd report to Caliente no later than 9:00.

JUST AN AVERAGE DAY

Everything was normal on the Tuesday before Thanksgiving, 1960. Tony left home at the usual time, but drove Virginia's convertible instead of his sedan, so he could have one of the mechanics at the track take care of some minor repairs. By now, Caliente operated like a small city, with its own systems. We had employees for everything from setting broken bones to translating for foreign dignitaries.

After a routine day at the office, Tony left Caliente at around 4:45, as usual. In those days, crossing the border was no problem: he pulled into his own driveway about half an hour later; again, as usual. In late November, it was already almost completely dark.

As he eased the long white convertible up his secluded driveway, two men wearing ski masks leaped from behind the 6-foot hedges with guns raised. They ordered Tony to stop the car, and before he could collect his wits, they'd pulled him from the car, bound and gagged him, shoved him into the trunk of his wife's white Cadillac and drove away.

Inside the house, Virginia and the girls were following their normal routine. Virginia was putting the final touches on the family dinner while Toni and Denise, then seven and five, washed their hands under the watchful eye of Juanita, the family maid. They were all waiting for Tony, and when he walked in the door, the girls would run into his arms, as always. Nobody heard a sound outside. Everything still seemed normal.

By 5:30, Virginia was getting worried. It wasn't like Tony to be late without calling. The girls were getting impatient, so Virginia went ahead and served them dinner. She'd wait and eat with Tony when he arrived.

When the phone rang at 5:45, she raced to answer it. He must be stuck in traffic. Or maybe the car broke down again.

Instead, it was a deep, male voice Virginia didn't recognize.

"Mrs. Alessio?" the Voice said politely. "We have Tony."

Understandably confused, Virginia replied,

"What?"

"We have your husband Tony," the Voice repeated. "We'll be getting back to you shortly on what we want for ransom."

RANSOM?

Terrified, Virginia tried to swallow her fear and collect her thoughts.

"I see. What do you want me to do?"

The Voice recited the address of a public phone in the La Mesa area, and told Virginia to drive there immediately. The phone would ring at 6:15, and she had better not be late. She would receive further instructions there. He warned her, "If you don't follow these instructions to the letter, you'll never see Tony alive again!"

Imagine the effect on a San Diego housewife. The line went dead. Virginia hung up the phone, eyes wide, hands shaking. Her daughters noticed.

"What's the matter, Mom?" they asked.

Virginia thought quickly, and told Juanita, "Quick, get the girls' coats. We have to leave."

She called a neighbor, asked her to take the kids. She gave Juanita the night off.

She arrived alone at the phone on time. The phone was ringing.

"Look behind the phone equipment," the Voice told her. "You'll see a note. We want this money right away, you understand?"

"Yes, sir," Virginia agreed, as she searched and found the note.

"We'll call you next at your house, " the Voice continued. "We want to talk to Johnny Alessio. Is that clear? And you'd better not call the police if you ever want to see your husband alive again."

"Yes, sir."

"That's a good girl. Now, you read that note and follow it to a 'T' and no monkey business. All we want is the money and you can have your Tony back in time for Thanksgiving."

The line went dead.

Hands shaking, Virginia read and re-read the note. They wanted $650,000 in small bills. That would be $6.5 million in 1998 dollars. The note concluded: "If you don't come up with the money in 24 hours, we'll start sending you Tony's ears and fingers."

How could she possibly get that kind of money together in 24 hours? How could anyone? They only had a few thousand in savings. Virginia got back in Tony's car and started crying.

A few hours later I got a call from Johnny. He asked if I'd talked to Tony. I had not.

"You'd better get over to his house, and don't say a word to anyone, not even Mardy," he told me.

I had no idea why Johnny was insisting. It was just a few days till Thanksgiving. We didn't have any big deals pending. I was afraid there had been some kind of accident. I walked into Tony's house, and all our other brothers were arriving simultaneously.

"What's up?" I ask.

And then Johnny gives us all the word, "Tony's been kidnapped." It was like a punch in the stomach. My little brother, kidnapped?

Johnny showed us the note, and warned us not to touch it. It was a nasty, frightening note, nothing you could ever be prepared for. Virginia was trying to be tough, but we could see she'd been crying. We all tried to think what to do, but we couldn't think straight.

❧

Now, it's 1960. We Alessios had been in San Diego most of our lives, and, then and now, we had many good friends. One of them was the Chief of Police, Mr. A.E. Jensen. Even though the kidnappers had said not to involve the police, we felt we had no choice. We called and asked him to come over to Tony's place, and he arrived without any more explanation.

When he got there, we told him what was going on. "This is bigger than my police force," he told us. "It's bigger than most city police departments in the country. We have to call in the FBI."

We were worried that with the FBI involved, there would be leaks to the press, but after a long discussion Chief Jensen persuaded us. Fresh in our minds was the recent kidnapping, just weeks before, of a member of the Coors family in Denver. In that case, the victim had been killed.

The same FBI team who had worked the Coors case was now in San Diego. Chief Jensen called them in. They arrived at Tony's around 11:00 p.m.. There must have been six or eight of them, with an Agent Price in charge.

We listened to the FBI agents, with all their experience. They insisted we not pay any ransom, because whatever the kidnappers were going to do, they'd do if we paid or not. The kidnappers had told Virginia they wanted to talk to Johnny, because he was the money man at the racetrack. When they did call back and speak with him, they insisted, "You just have the money when we tell you and where we tell you and everything will work out just fine."

We played along, while we tried to figure out who was behind this. Unless we had a clue who we were dealing with, the chances of getting Tony back would be slim. If they even thought we'd gone to the police or the FBI, it would mean the end of Tony. They warned us not just once, but many times.

Agent Price and the FBI team sat all the brothers down and asked a lot of questions about who we were and where we came from. We told them about our parents, and why we came to San Diego, and how hard we'd been working as a family. Chief Jensen explained about our national exposure as a result of Caliente and our various business interests. He pointed out we were front page news all over the West Coast.

We filled in the agents on some other information we had heard. About a year before there had been talk of establishing Las Vegas-style casinos in Tijuana. Since Tijuana is closer than Vegas to Los Angeles, we had learned that this subject was of considerable concern to the Nevada casino operators.

"We heard some of the guys from Vegas were down, looking over spots like Rosarito Beach and Ensenada, and some of the bars and clubs in Tijuana," Johnny told the agents. "But they never came to see us. We weren't too concerned because we knew the Mexican government didn't want open gambling."

"You opposed it, though?" Price asked.

"Naturally. It would have cut badly into our business at the track, but mainly, we wanted to cooperate with the Mexican government," Johnny explained.

"There were no threats?"

"No," Johnny assured Price. "Believe me, I'm not holding anything back where it concerns my brother."

Next, we discussed Tony's car. Finding the white convertible would give the authorities a starting point for their investigation, but if they put out an "all points" alert, it might tip off the media or the kidnappers that the police were involved, and that would jeopardize Tony. Jensen and Price agreed to go with a "confidential alert," meaning patrol officers should report seeing the car but do nothing to stop it.

Because Johnny had already spoken with the kidnappers once, the FBI turned to him as the family spokesman. The rest of us stayed on hand to do whatever we could. We were all worried sick.

An FBI agent was stationed inside Tony's house, guarding Virginia and the girls around the clock. They arranged to record all future phone calls. They set up a short-wave broadcast system so they could communicate with other agents outside the house, around the city and in Los Angeles. The inside agents would also advise on further negotiations.

"Let's make sure we all understand one thing," Johnny told Price and Jensen. "Paying the money or catching these punks means nothing to us when it comes to Tony. The only thing that matters is getting him back alive and well."

Price nodded agreement. He assured us that their investigations would in no way hinder our negotiations for Tony's release.

I still had some doubts. "Virginia is real upset, and so are my brothers and me," I said. "It was our idea to call you in. If this gets fouled up, we're going to be in a tough spot with Tony's wife and kids, not to mention the rest of the family."

Price quickly pointed out that based on other recent major kidnappings, the odds were about 50-50 that Tony would be returned unharmed, whether or not the ransom was paid. He cited records going back to the Lindbergh baby in 1932. In 20 major kidnappings, 11 victims had not been found alive. In cases where the victims had not been safely returned, police involvement was not a factor in the decision by the kidnappers to kill. In several cases, victims were killed without any reason while ransom negotiations were in progress.

"We won't prevent a payment," Price told us, "but remember this: once the money is paid, all you've got is the word of a criminal that he'll release your brother. With a possible death sentence hanging over his head, there's not much incentive to let your brother go, unless he thinks he's going to get away with it."

We could have done without that grim reminder, but the Alessios had faced long odds before and come out winners. That was the story of our whole family. And I knew Tony. He was sharp. He was probably feeding the kidnappers a big snow-job right now, while we were all talking and worrying ourselves sick.

By midnight or so, the FBI had men and equipment in place at Tony's. Just after 1:00 a.m. Wednesday, the kidnappers called.

Johnny picked up the phone. They wanted the ransom money by noon today—less than 12 hours away. Johnny tried to buy time and feel out the kidnapper about what would happen if we didn't come up with the money. All this was to keep him talking so we could trace the call and get his voice on tape, so we could have some clues about who these people were. The FBI decided the call came from a pay phone in Los Angeles.

The night dragged on. Johnny talked to the kidnappers two or three more times, and told them it would be impossible to gather so much cash so quickly. It was the day before Thanksgiving.

"If you want your brother back and you follow instructions, you'll have Tony back one minute before midnight tonight."

Johnny pleaded with the kidnappers. "We just can't get that much money so fast." This was a negotiation tactic. We'd already talked to Arnie Smith at National Bank, and he'd promised us as much cash as we needed. In fact, the money was already being counted and marked, but we were following the FBI's advice. They were the pros, and we knew we had to listen.

Back at my house, things were a little difficult, because my sons, who still lived at home, were seeing me come and go at all hours. They knew something was up. Larry, the eldest, was really curious, but I explained that I couldn't talk to him right now; it was too dangerous.

I told Mardy a little more, but not too much. It seemed like the less they knew, the better, though the tension and the heartache were about the worst I'd ever known. Just thinking about my baby brother being shot or tortured by those SOBs was enough to drive me crazy.

The kidnappers called again later on Wednesday morning.

"I know I can get you $200,000 in small bills, " Johnny told them. "It's going to be a big bundle, though."

"Get yourself a duffel bag," the guy recommended. "And no funny business. If we don't get the cash, Tony is dead."

"I can have your money by this afternoon. Where do you want it?"

"We'll call later. If we even smell a cop, you know what will happen."

This call came from San Diego, and the voice was different.

Wednesday afternoon dragged on and on. The money had been counted, marked, and stuffed in a duffel bag. Johnny paced the floor at Tony's like a caged animal. The rest of us tried to go about our daily business like nothing was wrong. We wanted the rest of the world to think everything was just fine. No problems here!

⚜

To keep up appearances, I kept to my routine. I went for coffee with some of the businessmen near my office at Alessio Motors, just like always. It was a real strain to seem chipper, and laugh at everyone's jokes. I kept sneaking looks at my watch, to see when I could check in with Johnny.

One of my buddies even commented, "You don't look like yourself, Angelo. Don't you feel good?"

I assured him I felt fine.

Five o'clock came and went, and nothing happened. I went home, tried to eat dinner with Mardy and the kids, and had no appetite. I excused myself, told them I had to go to a meeting, and left.

Back at Tony's, Johnny was a nervous wreck. He'd told the FBI he was going to deliver the money, and no one could talk him out of it.

"We can't give you any coverage if you make the drop, " Agent Price warned him. "It would be too dangerous."

Johnny saw no other choice. "I'm the guy they asked for," he reminded everyone. "I'm the guy they've been talking to. They know what I look like. I'm not thrilled about dealing with these bastards, but it's my job to do. I'll take care of it."

Finally, just before 8 o'clock, the phone rang.

"You ready?" the voice asked.

"I have the money, just like you said," Johnny replied.

The caller told him to use Tony's other Cadillac, take the money, and drive immediately to a certain phone booth in downtown San Diego. There, he'd find written instructions. Once he had these, he was to proceed without stopping to an address on the paper.

"You'll be followed," the caller warned. "If you make any bad moves, the deal's off and Tony's dead."

Johnny tried to repeat the instructions, but the guy hung up.

The FBI agents told Johnny to memorize the written instructions then drop the paper on the floor of the phone booth like he was in a panic. They'd have someone in disguise pick it up. They had fake sailors all ready to use for just this kind of situation. The FBI really knew their stuff.

Johnny left as he'd been told. He drove carefully through the pitch black November night. An accident, even a fender-bender, could spell disaster. The kidnappers might suspect some kind of trick, or a signal to the police.

Meanwhile, back at Tony's house, a thousand troubling thoughts ran through my head. Was Tony still alive? The kidnappers had never let us speak with him. Would the money buy his release?

As promised, the directions were in the phone booth. Johnny was instructed to drive to a parking lot in Los Angeles, at Hollywood Boulevard and Bronson Avenue. He was to leave Tony's car unlocked and walk away.

The FBI and police seemed hopeful. They had about two hours to set up for the delivery in L.A. It seemed that the kidnappers were feeling confident that they had things under control and that we were following instructions. Maybe we really would get Tony back safe and sound.

Still, it was a long drive to Hollywood. Anywhere along the freeway, the kidnappers could force Johnny, in his distinctive white Cadillac, off the road, and make off with the money. The FBI and police were following him along the way, taking note of any car that stayed around too long.

Agents at Tony's house kept the rest of us up to date. The tension was unbelievable. We had no idea who we'd hear from next: Johnny, the kidnappers, the police, the FBI, a well-meaning friend just calling to say, "Happy Thanksgiving." Time has never passed so slowly.

THE MONEY DROP

We tried to comfort Virginia and her daughters, and assure her everything would be okay, but she knew we were as worried as she was. This situation, and our brother, were in the hands of God, and there was nothing more we could do. Johnny was giving it his all; he put himself on the line. Who knows, they might nab him, too. Would they keep their promise to release Tony? Maybe he could identify them. Maybe they'd be desperate enough to silence the one potential witness who might put them in the gas chamber.

We learned why the kidnappers had picked that particular drop-off point. "The Santa Claus parade is going on tonight, " the L.A. FBI chief told Price. "The streets are jammed."

This Hollywood parade was filled with movie and television personalities. Spectators came from all over Los Angeles. Shops stayed open late, and the crowds would make it difficult for agents to follow whoever picked up the ransom.

"There are too many variables, " Price explained. All the FBI could do was to keep the car and the ransom money under observation. Maybe someone would pick up the duffel bag. Maybe someone would drive off in the Cadillac.

Johnny knew nothing of this. He parked the car, left the keys in the ignition, and walked away without looking back. His own bodyguard, who had followed him from San Diego, picked him up and they drove to FBI headquarters in L.A. When he arrived, Johnny called Tony's house, so we knew at least that he was safe.

The FBI and police observers kept watch, and soon someone came by, picked up the duffel bag and ran to a waiting car. Within minutes, he had disappeared into the holiday traffic.

Back at Tony's house, we waited tensely. Less than half an hour remained before midnight. We all paced the floor, chain smoking, scared and helpless.

Had it been a mistake bringing in the FBI? What had it gotten us? We'd turned over the money to these people, and like Agent Price had warned us, we had only the word of criminals that Tony would be released. They could just as easily take the money, kill Tony, and disappear forever.

Ninety minutes after the ransom money was picked up, the telephone rang at Tony's. It was just before midnight. Virginia snatched up the receiver.

"He's all yours," said the mysterious male voice. "You'll find him at the Cozy Inn Motel on El Cajon Boulevard."

It was just a few miles from Tony's house. Virginia jumped in a car with FBI agents; I followed in my car. Would Tony be there? Would he be alive? Price, Jensen, and

Cozy Inn where Tony was held during his kidnapping, 11/1960

more agents converged on the scene from the downtown FBI headquarters. Word was flashed to Johnny at FBI headquarters in L.A.

Within minutes, the Cozy Inn Motel swarmed with investigators. Its dazed owner, Donald Quam, was bombarded with questions.

Tony was in one of the units, still blindfolded and handcuffed to a bed, but otherwise unharmed. He and Virginia had a joyful, but tearful, reunion.

"I'm okay, Honey," Tony reassured his nearly hysterical wife. "They treated me okay. How much money did you have to give them?"

That was our Tony. Against all odds, safe and sound, and home for Thanksgiving, a day I'll never forget.

Part III

The Midas Touch

CHAPTER TWELVE

Who Done It?

Here's what we found out. Apparently the kidnappers had followed Tony home, and bundled him into the trunk of the Cadillac. They drove around for a while, then switched to another car, and drove to the Cozy Inn where they had reserved a three-room cottage. That's where Tony had been for all those tense hours.

The weirdest thing is that The Cozy Inn was just across the street from where I had coffee that Wednesday morning, trying to pretend to my buddies that everything was normal.

Meanwhile, two kidnappers played cards in one room, while another kept an eye on Tony, bound and blindfolded. Tony talked to his guard, who had a mean mouth and an ugly way about him. At one point, Tony almost convinced him to take $50,000 and let him go. He was also listening to the card players out front.

Tony learned that they were connected to a guy who had tried to cheat us with a fake 5-10 ticket at the racetrack. This wasn't uncommon. A lot of people tried it, and some were pretty good at it. They'd alter their ticket so a seven looked like some other number, for instance.

One of these cheaters was named Marrone. He was from Alaska, and liked to play the horses, especially the 5-10. We didn't know much else about him, except he was a heavy bettor, and then one time he came in with a forged ticket.

Now, of course we had security at Caliente. We had our own police department. If people got out of line, we'd put them in our little jail for a few hours, then let them out. We never kept them overnight.

Marrone made a big fuss when we brought him in with his fake ticket. He insisted it was good, but we knew better. We gave him a choice: spend some time in our jail, or get out. He left, but not before he threatened us, "I'll get you Italians sooner or later."

We got many empty threats from cheaters like him; we ran them off and didn't think too much about it. This guy was more dangerous than most, though. Later, the cops told us Marrone was an ex-convict who'd served time for murder. This guy, with his grudge against the Alessios, was the mastermind of the whole kidnapping operation.

We got a lot of this information from Tony, who had been listening to his captors the whole time he was their hostage.

His most nervous moments came after they had picked up the ransom. After Marrone made the pick-up he went to some secret place and started counting the money. It took a long time with all those small bills, but at some point he realized it was far less than half a million dollars. He called the motel and told his partners.

Tony could hear them talking in the next room, calling us a bunch of "cheap dagos," and cussing us out. Eventually, though, they decided to take the money and run, and let our brother go.

Later, the investigators learned the kidnappers had divided the money up, and that Marrone had shorted his partners in crime, taking at least $100,000 for himself and leaving them to divide the rest. The FBI wouldn't have known who the ringleader was, except Tony recognized the voice and remembered the name of the guy who'd try to fake a 5-10 ticket.

CHEATERS NEVER PROSPER...

...And crooks are dumb. Tony's brilliant memory of the crooked Marrone provided the first clue to solving the crime. Tony also provided aural descriptions of Marrone's henchmen.

One had a Texas accent. The other sounded like he was just a kid. They had been left in charge of Tony while Marrone collected the ransom in L.A.

Once Tony was securely free and at home, the story became front page news in papers all over the country, and in Mexico too, where we were also well known. "Alessio Kidnapped and Released," the headlines read.

The Texan turned out to be a flamboyant character who wore a fringed leather jacket. He took his payoff and went down to Mexicali on a tequila binge. He got pie-eyed drunk and threw his money around, especially with the women.

The ladies in the bar were naturally curious. "Where'd you get the dinero?" they asked the drunken Texan.

"We had to kidnap a guy and take his money," he bragged.

Some of the women put two and two together. "Hey, that's the Alessios!" they concluded, right before they went to the police. The Texan had by then headed back to San Diego, still drunk on tequila.

The Mexican police called the FBI, and passed along the tip. The FBI staked out the San Diego bus station downtown on Broadway. They recognized their man immediately: a drunk in a fringed leather jacket with a Texas accent.

"You're under arrest for kidnapping," they announced.

In his condition, it didn't take much to persuade him to spill the beans in exchange for a lighter sentence. He was upset because he felt shortchanged on his share. The Texan told the agents how he'd hooked up with Marrone, and about Maronne's wife, and about the kid. He told them where Marrone lived in L.A. He gave them a description of Marrone's car.

The feds staked out Marrone's house, but he didn't show. They put out a bulletin, and the Los Angeles police looked for his car, and when they spotted it on the freeway, Marrone gave up without a fight. Later, they located his wife, but neither of them would talk.

In the meantime, they found the other member of the gang. He was just a kid, who had worked in a store in Chula Vista. He still was holding about $78,000. Marrone's share turned up when the FBI searched the house where he'd been staying and found

Frank Marrone, the mastermind behind Tony's kidnapping

about $100,000 inside a refrigerator door. We ended up getting all but $22,000 of the ransom money back.

Marrone was convicted, and later extradited back to Alaska where he served another 20-30 years for violating parole. While he was in prison, he smuggled out letters threatening Tony.

"You think you got away with it? We'll get you sooner or later," he would write. Tony turned the letters over to the FBI, and Marrone got another 10 years added to his sentence. As far as we know, he's still serving time in Alaska.

We never did get the last $22,000 back. At one point we tried to deduct it from our taxes, but the IRS and the Franchise Tax Board in California both turned us down. To this day, the missing money has never turned up. Every bill was marked, so anyone who tried to spend it would be in deep trouble.

It was a horrifying situation, but it turned out as well as anyone could expect. We did what the kidnappers asked, we worked with the FBI and we got our Tony back for Thanksgiving.

When all the publicity came out, we were all really worried about our children. Maybe there really had been someone else behind the scenes. Maybe the people in Las Vegas actually were sending us a message.

By now, of course, we had all remembered Mother's warnings. She'd worried about our kids, but in reality it was one of her boys who was taken. From then on, all the Alessios became very security conscious.

That Thanksgiving, though, we all had a lot to be grateful for.

Tony as pictured in Official Detective Stories *magazine (March, 1961) as part of the cover story*

CHAPTER THIRTEEN

The Racing News

Tony was kidnapped near the end of 1960, but that whole year, and for some time before, many amazing, and much more positive events had been happening to the Alessio family. We'd only been running Caliente since 1947, but opportunities were opening up too rapidly for me to keep track.

Our successes had earned us a reputation for having the Midas Touch. It seemed every time someone had a new deal, they wanted us to participate because all our investments were making big money. We tried to remain conservative and careful, but it was also hard to say "no."

You may recall that we had gone into business with the Funk brothers, the Arizona family who had brought greyhound racing to Caliente. That enterprise had been profitable for all, so when they approached us about building a new track in Phoenix, we looked into it.

A new track would cost about four million dollars. We Alessios didn't want to front that much out of our pockets, but Dave Funk was a promoter if ever there was one. He suggested we sell debentures. I'd never heard of such a thing, but our lawyers assured us the plan was legitimate.

The debentures were worth $25 apiece; for every debenture purchased the investor would receive 25 shares of race track stock, worth a penny each. So for every 25 shares of stock, we'd get $250, and return a debenture worth $.25. These were legally registered with the state of Arizona.

At first, the money came flying in. Everyone wanted to own a piece of a race track. Soon we had collected well over a million dollars, but later, the debentures were harder to sell. Albert Funk met with some big

investors from Phoenix, Bud Antel and Ben Kellerman. They were in
the produce business, and bought a substantial quantity of debentures.

We were getting close to the necessary four million investment
when I got a call from Dave Funk.

"You better get over here a week from today. We're putting up the
first piece of steel for the new track. The governor's coming for the big
ground-breaking."

"Dave," I protested, "we don't have all the money yet!"

"Don't worry," he assured me. "Once we get that steel up they're not
going to come back and take it down."

That bothered me. We didn't do business that way. But Dave was
determined that we had to get started, so I went over for the ceremony.

It wasn't long, though, before we started running into more money
problems. Luckily, Antel and Kellerman lent us most of what we
needed, and so they ended up as major shareholders. Now there were
three groups in control: the Funks, the Alessios, Antel and Kellerman.

Bud and Ben had confidence in us, and promised to back us at
shareholder meetings. They gave us their proxies, and so we ran things
at the new track and began bringing in good money. We decided to
build another track in Tucson. We had built up a surplus, and didn't
need to sell debentures, but I was never really comfortable with the
third-third-third ownership arrangement.

We started getting calls from some of our suppliers complaining
they weren't getting paid by the Funks, who were there in Arizona.

I flew over to meet with them.

"Oh, I'm paying the bills," Dave told me.

Then why were the suppliers calling me? Dave opened a desk
drawer, and there were all the checks, filled out, signed, and waiting to
be mailed!

"That's not how we do things," I told him. I brought Johnny up to
speed, and he worked it out so everyone was paid. We Alessios never
messed with our credit.

About two years into this arrangement, Bud Antel had become the
biggest lettuce grower in the Southwest. I was in his office one day when
he cornered the entire U.S. market. His buddy Kellerman was less flamboyant. Unbeknownst to us, Bud Antel and the Funk brothers were getting closer. Bud wanted to get more involved with the racetrack, and so

at one shareholders meeting he voted his and Kellerman's stock with the Funks.

That shook Johnny and me up. We foresaw trouble ahead. We checked with our accountant, then waited until the next meeting a month later.

We announced to our partners that we'd been in Arizona long enough, and wanted to concentrate our efforts back at Caliente. We wanted to run our dogs there, and we wanted to sell out our shares.

Bud agreed to buy us out. He offered us a million dollars.

Johnny and I stepped outside to talk it over.

Back in the meeting, I told Bud, "Okay, we'll take your million dollars."

"Come to my office this afternoon, and I'll give you a check for $750,00. You'll get the rest in six months," he replied.

We'd gotten what we wanted from Arizona—made money, made a lot of friends. But we remembered what our father had told us long ago, "Never turn your back on profit."

We went back to Caliente and put all our energy there. But when the final quarter million came due, Antel started making excuses. Fortunately his partner Ben Kellerman was a real fine fellow.

When I told him, "Ben, I'm afraid I'm going to have to take you and Antel to court," he gave me his word he'd get the final payment for us. He promised that if Antel didn't make the payment, he'd do it himself.

Six more months went by, but we finally got our money, and walked away happy from Arizona. Meanwhile, the Funks now had five dog tracks in Arizona, so they left Caliente, and that was fine with us.

NOISES FROM NEW MEXICO

Somewhere in this hectic period, I got a call from Arnie Smith. Anytime Arnie called, we'd drop everything, because he had always done the same for us. He was a genuine tycoon by now, with a commercial fishing fleet, taxi cabs all over California, the Westgate development company, and of course his National Bank.

Still, he always made time for the Alessios, just as he'd made Johnny's original opportunity at Banco del Pacifico. When I wanted to see him, I'd go right up to his office on the 25th floor of the bank, and he'd interrupt whatever he was doing.

This time, Arnie was in a big meeting, but his secretary sent me into another, private room. Arnie was always a sharp dresser, big and good looking, and he strode in wearing his trademark tan suit.

"Angelo," he said, "I've got a favor to ask. You've gotta go over to New Mexico and take over the Ruidoso racetrack."

I shook my head, "Arnie, we've already got too much going on. "

"I know," he said, "but I need your help."

Ruidoso was one of the most famous quarter horse tracks in the United States. It had the highest purse of all quarter horse tracks, a million dollar race once a year.

This purse didn't come out of the operators' pocket. The deal was more like a fraternity, where each horse breeder would enter his horse in the race when it was still just a foal. The owner would then contribute a fixed amount every year to maintain his horse's entry. Like a high stakes poker game, the owners anted up to build the million dollar purse.

Ruidoso (which means noisy, referring to the nearby Ruidoso River), is about 3000 feet up in the Sacramento Mountains of New Mexico, 100 miles north of El Paso, Texas and Ciudad Juárez in the Mexican state of Chihuahua. It's a beautiful setting and a refreshing spot for the Texans to escape the muggy summer heat. The million dollar race got lots of media coverage. The Texans took the opportunity for a tax deductible vacation, show off a little, and run their horses.

Arnie wanted us to take over because one of his partners was trying to run the track as well as his mortgage and insurance businesses in Los Angeles and San Francisco. Arnie needed for his partner to concentrate on the California ventures and asked the Alessios to manage the place.

I told him I'd go look it over. I talked it over with Johnny, Russ and Tony and we decided to tackle it, to make a few dollars and do a favor for Arnie Smith.

It was a quaint little track, but it needed remodeling. I told Arnie, "We just don't have the money to go in and do the improvements it needs." The track and clubhouse needed to better suit the clientele.

Arnie assured me that if we'd fix the place up, he'd see we got the money. So we made ourselves popular in New Mexico without spending our own money. Once everything was running well, we put Johnny's son Bud and his son-in-law Al Rosa in charge, and they did a good job there. We had the biggest race in the world, and many visiting dignitaries every year. I couldn't begin to name all the important Texans, but you'd never have known they were multi-millionaires because they all wore cowboy boots, and some of them still had horse manure on them!

Unfortunately, we also had to deal with flaky New Mexican politicians. They'd come around, patting us on the back, and congratulate us on the good job we were doing. But when it came time to enact new rules and regulations to improve horse racing, they just vanished into thin air.

One night, a member of the racing board came in. I made sure he was well taken care of at the Turf Club. He was putting on a big show for his two young female companions. He and I talked about some action taking place the next day at the state legislature.

"Angelo," he promised me, "you boys have done such a good job, there's no way that bill won't pass." He didn't even show up the next day for the vote.

Still, we had become so successful we started getting pushed around by some powerful New Mexican business interests. Some had owned the track in the past. They decided they wanted it back.

We could see we'd have an uphill battle against these influential locals, so when they made us an offer, we decided it was time to get out. We sold our position and left with a profit.

Chapter Fourteen

Back Across the Borderline

A hundred miles south of Ruidoso, right across the Rio Grande from El Paso, Texas, Ciudad Juárez is a busy Mexican border town not unlike Tijuana. It made perfect sense, then, for the Mexican government to look to the Alessios when they wanted to put a racetrack in that part of the country.

They wanted to draw more tourists, and also to have access to the prosperous Texan horse breeders across the river. Oddly, with its long and illustrious equestrian history, Texas was not a big horse racing state. They had outlawed pari-mutuel betting in 1937, and it was not legalized again until 1987. This was certainly one of the reasons Ruidoso had become so popular with the Texans.

We had, of course, made many friends among the Texan horse-breeding community, and they were elated when we told them we'd gotten a permit to open a racetrack in Juárez. We already had a successful working relationship with the Mexican government, and we signed a contract with the powerful Mexican labor union guaranteeing a certain number of working days to our employees.

We knew the government and the union were expecting a real nice track. But this time, I thought Johnny might have overdone it. Instead of letting me build a practical track of wood or steel, he got carried away and decided to build the Taj Majal of race tracks. He was counting on all the Texas business, and wanted to build one of the greatest tracks in North America.

I admit it was a spectacular facility, all done in concrete with first class grandstand, club house and turf. It took a year, and $9 million, to build. The seed money came from Caliente and its investors, most of whom lived in Mexico City. We didn't use any Alessio money, but we did all the work.

The Texans, of course, had to bring their horses through an inspection station at the border. In the beginning, we got some fine horses; we also had the dog track, and all went well. The purses and the crowds were good, and it galloped along like that for about nine months.

For no apparent reason, the Mexican immigration officials at the line started hassling the owners when they were bringing their horses in. The Americans, quite naturally, complained. Some had to wait for hours. It's not healthy for highly bred horses to be penned up like that in the Mexican sun. Little by little, the Texans stopped coming.

We couldn't seem to correct the situation. People wondered aloud how we could allow such a thing to happen. Based on our lengthy relationship with the Mexican government, we had assumed they would keep their word. We figured the Texans would understand if the politicians messed up. Word was spreading, and we couldn't stop the bad publicity.

We couldn't go in and tell Mexican bureaucrats what to do in their own country. We wanted to stop racing horses and just run the dogs, but we were contracted to employ 2,000 people. The foreign book and the dogs were what kept us afloat.

Johnny went to Mexico City, reminding people of our deal and asking for support, but no one would accept responsibility for making the necessary changes.

A race track depends on the quality of the horses. Better horses draw more sophisticated and well-heeled bettors. Savvy bettors judge the quality of horses instantly. We tried to keep the quality up by bringing in horses from Caliente—they were already "imported."

The situation continued to deteriorate, though. Soon, mordida raised its jaws to put the "little bite" on everyone trying to cross the border. Customs inspectors changed frequently, and often the horsevan drivers didn't have enough dinero to pay the requested bribes.

I was spending a lot of my time in Juárez, and John came when he could. Tony and Russ were stuck at Caliente, trying to keep that operation on course. We had a good general manager, who had worked for us at Caliente; we tried new promotions, even changed ad agencies. Nothing worked. The Texans were incensed at the way they had been treated by immigration. We never could get them back in the same numbers.

We had signed a 15-year concession with the Mexican government; when it came up for renewal, we actually did decide to re-apply. Johnny gets the credit there. He spent a lot of time with the big politicians and lawyers in Mexico City. But soon, a new group of investors from Mexico City came around; they knew business had dropped off and they could pick up the track for a bargain price.

We negotiated with them for half a year, until finally we decided we'd be better off putting all that effort into other ventures. We sold out. Juárez was the first Alessio investment where we walked away with only a modest profit. But it was nice for a change to eliminate all the travel, come back home, and check on my own nest.

HAPPIER TIMES IN MEXICO

Mardy and I, who celebrated our 60th wedding anniversary in the year 2000, raised our family and always maintained our principal home in San Diego. But we also made a point of traveling, and we saw much of the world.

Since those long ago picnics with my father in Tijuana, and through our whole wonderful association with Caliente, I had maintained a soft spot in my heart for Mexico. Mardy and I had a friend, Dick Grahalva, who had done very well as a car dealer in San Diego. He had discovered a little Pacific coast fishing village called Puerto Vallarta.

Dick was a wheeler-dealer. He had built a home for himself there, and a couple more for resale. He had opened a few little businesses; jewelry stores and a restaurant. Starting around 1955, Mardy and I would go down and visit him there. It was a lovely place—quiet, clean, almost unknown to foreigners.

Today, of course, Puerto Vallarta is a major tourist destination, with beach front hotels and condominiums. It must have been sometime in the early 1960s that Dick showed us a lot in an area called Gringo Gulch, overlooking the ocean above the tiny downtown area. At that time, maybe four other American families had houses there, as well as my old pal from Caliente, Elizabeth Taylor.

Liz had discovered Puerto Vallarta after she'd gotten together with Richard Burton. They were the world's most famous and scandalous couple in 1963, when he went there to star with Ava Gardner and Debra Kerr in the filmed version of Tennessee Williams' "Night of the Iguana," directed by John Huston.

Liz would not be separated from her new love, and accompanied Burton to Puerto Vallarta for the long months of filming. The world press followed along. The film crew built generators, water tanks, docks, pumps; bungalows to house the crew, a restaurant-bar, and sets which remain today as picturesque ruins. This event transformed Puerto Vallarta, and literally put it on the map for decades to come.

Liz bought a house in Gringo Gulch, and settled in there. Later, Burton bought a house across the street, and they built a bridge connecting the two love nests across Zaragoza Street. To this day, this is a Puerto Vallarta landmark.

The lot Dick showed us was close to town, with a breathtaking view of Banderas Bay. An American owned the land but had never developed it. I casually remarked to Dick, "If I ever move down here, I'd sure like to have that lot."

Weeks later, back in San Diego, I got a call. It was Dick.

"You know that lot you looked at? You don't know it, but you now own it. I went and bought it for you."

HUH? "How much do I owe you," I stammered. He gave me a figure—I think it was about $7500.

I told him I'd come down to bring him the money. I started getting excited. Mardy and I went back down, and then things started getting out of hand.

First, the lot was not really buildable. It went almost straight up and down on a cliff. "Let's start talking about the kind of house you want," Dick suggested.

"Wait just a minute," I replied.

Dick was, as I mentioned, a wheeler-dealer, who had built homes and businesses here in Puerto Vallarta. He called in one of the best local builders, Guillermo Construction. They had built the sets for "Night of the Iguana," and worked with an excellent architect.

In the states, of course, to build anything you need architectural plans, engineering reports, and approvals from dozens of government departments before you can even begin. Then you've got endless inspections and approvals and permits before the work can be completed and inhabited. It can take years, not even counting the months for the actual construction.

Things are different in Mexico. The guys asked me, "What do you want?"

I looked at Mardy, and shrugged. She looked back, equally at a loss. "We want a truly Mexican house that fits in with this beautiful town," I finally blurted.

Fine, they said. The architect pulled out a piece of paper, and sketched out the lot, including the steep incline.

"Here's what we'll build," he said, while drawing the top floor on a second sheet of paper. "Here's the kitchen. Here's the dining room. Here's the front room, and we'll put a balcony way out to here. Upstairs, we'll put some bedrooms.

"That's the top floor. Now, here, we'll put the stairway. On the lower floor we'll put two big bedrooms, and your master bedroom, with an open-air bathroom, and another patio. The gardener will be here, and the maid's quarters, a bathroom, a living room. How does that look?"

"I'd like to see the plans, " I replied doubtfully.

"Oh," the architect assured me. "We don't use plans. This is what we're going to build. It will be a big house, about 3,000 square feet." He gave me the measurement in meters, but I got the picture.

I tried to protest, but "No, no, no, this is what it's gonna be. This is the way we're going to build it."

The builder offered to show me some of his previous work around town. They were beautiful houses. I talked with the owners, and they assured me that yes, if he said it, that's what he'd do.

I gave in. "How much am I going to owe you for this house," I inquired.

"I'll build it for you for $28,000."

I thought I might be dreaming. Mardy and I had bought houses and traded up a few times in San Diego. This kind of place would cost ten or twenty times as much back there.

"All I'll ask you," the builder continued, "is to send me $1,000 a week while I'm building, and a little money right now for materials."

The architect, it turned out, owned a furniture store. Most of the furnishings were included in the $28,000.

What could I say but "Let's go."

Now this had been a sudden and completely unexpected transaction. Mardy and I were set to leave for Africa on a 30-day hunting safari. Dick Grahalva lived right down the street, though, and promised to keep an eye on things for me. He watched the house as if it were his own.

The safari was terrific, but when we got back we couldn't wait to check out our new Mexican hacienda. When we finally walked in, we could not believe our eyes.

Everything was perfect; just the way we wanted it, except for a single tiny detail. Mardell noticed one door that didn't have an arch over it. We mentioned it to the builder, and while we were downstairs looking over the rest of the house, four guys were chiseling the plaster. By the time we got back upstairs, the doorway was arched.

Outside, a magnificent and essential brick retaining wall held the backfill. In the states, it would have cost between $50,000 and $100,000. Here, it was included in the $28,000 price.

In all, the total construction amounted to more like 4,000 square feet, 30 percent more than the original estimate, but the price stayed the same: $28,000 plus the lot. Our Puerto Vallarta home, with its huge porch overlooking the city and the bay, is still one of the most beautiful houses in Gringo Gulch.

CHAPTER FIFTEEN

Constructing the Future, Building on the Past

For more than 100 years the Hotel del Coronado has been one of San Diego's most recognizable landmarks. It had been hosting visiting dignitaries since even before the Alessios arrived in San Diego, and had become even more famous in 1958, when Marilyn Monroe, Jack Lemmon, and Tony Curtis arrived to star in Billy Wilder's classic "Some Like It Hot." In the speakeasy days of the 20s and 30s, it had a close relationship with the hotel/spa at Caliente. It's now a national historic site.

Our racing associates, the Funk brothers, bought beach front acreage along the Silver Strand, adjacent to the Hotel Del. They had development plans, but got stuck with some back taxes in Arizona. When they were about to lose the property, they called me to see if we would take it over.

We jumped at the opportunity, and ended up paying $100,000 for 35 acres of prime beach front. Our idea was to put up a "new Hotel Del," not a high-rise, but a rambling beach resort. I worked with an architect and had him put together a scale model on a 4' x 8' piece of plywood.

I began taking this around town, showing it off to drum up financing. The original owner of the hotel, Elisha Babcock, had died, and the hotel was in the hands of his estate trustees. Their attorney, Mr. Jacobs, lived in Kansas City, but had his own cabaña at the hotel, where he liked to spend the summer.

By this time, the late 1950s, the hotel was looking a little shabby. The absentee owners didn't do much to maintain it.

Unexpectedly, I got a call from Mr. Jacobs, inviting me to his San Diego office for coffee. I didn't know what to expect, so I brought my architectural model with me. He asked me how advanced our project was.

I told him we were well aware we'd be going into competition with the legendary "Del," and so were not rushing into anything.

Jacobs asked me not to make any deals right away. He wanted to talk about selling the hotel. I was surprised, but kept a poker face. I told him I'd talk to my partners.

He went back to Kansas City. I talked to my brothers, who were as astonished as I was. "They want to sell us the Hotel Del because they're afraid of our project," I told them. We were definitely interested.

I called Jacobs, and told him next time he was in town we'd like to meet. I didn't make an offer. We talked about the condition of the hotel, a massive, wooden structure built in the last century. It would need a major face lift. He seemed concerned about his private cabaña. He wanted it available for the rest of his life. Since he was about 75 years old, I told him that shouldn't be too much of a problem. We didn't get too detailed about the purchase price, but he begged me not to start our competing project, and I promised we wouldn't.

We didn't want to have that huge hotel appraised; it would simply cost too much. Time passed, and Jacobs called again. He was ready to take an offer. I conferred with my brothers and our accountant Bob Mansfield and got the go-ahead, providing I could get a good deal.

After interminable preliminaries, Jacobs handed me a piece of paper with their price: $2.5 million.

"We don't have that much cash," I told him, "but we do have good credit."

"That, I already know," he assured me.

I called Arnie Smith and told him the deal. "Grab it," he replied.

Bob Mansfield and I went out again, and walked through the facilities. I didn't want to make a mistake. It looked good. I made the deal. It closed in March, 1960.

Now we owned a genuine San Diego historical landmark. Johnny stepped in, and we began the long, expensive process of remodeling. Johnny never needed a blueprint, he just knew what he wanted.

We contracted with McKee Construction, a major depositor at Arnie Smith's National Bank. We always liked to stay within our "family" of friends, people we knew and knew we could trust. Unfortunately, the funds for the remodeling, which cost around a million dollars, ended up causing us major problems. We borrowed from Caliente and some Mexican lenders—took out regular loans, paid them back with interest, but apparently Bob Mansfield, our longtime, trusted account, didn't enter these correctly in the Alessio books.

The remodeling, though, was totally correct. We tried to refurbish the worn out stuff, and still maintain the historic character of this grand old hotel. We had to be careful, because it was such a part of the community that many people took a proprietary interest in it. They felt they owned the Hotel Del.

Some were retired Navy captains and admirals who lived in the hotel. They gave us a lot of flack. The hotel has a wonderful, wrap-around porch, and it was lined with ancient rocking chairs. They were practically falling apart, so we decided to replace the rocker part. The old-timers gave us holy hell.

"How dare you ruin that chair? That's an antique, you dope. I've been sitting in that chair for the last 40 years. Who gave you the right to destroy my chair," and so forth. All we could do was listen politely.

McKee Construction was handling landscaping, moving sea walls and sand, when I got an emergency call.

"You'd better get over here right away," the foreman insisted. "Someone's going to file an injunction about a palm tree."

One of the retired Naval officers had worked himself up into a frenzy. Every morning when he walked his dog, the dog would lift his leg on this beautiful old palm tree. I assured him we wouldn't hurt the tree, we were just moving it a little closer to the ocean.

It seemed like everyone had their little piece of territory to protect. When we came in, there was some open space in the main lobby that wasn't in much use. Downstairs were the original bar and dining room, with a small dance floor. They really were more of a display for the merchants downstairs, where there were a clothing store and a barber shop.

Johnny decided to install a similar, intimate bar in the main lobby, more accessible for guests when they came into the hotel. Many of them didn't even realize the downstairs bar existed.

When we started working on the new one, no one said a word. They didn't know what we were doing, because there were so many changes and so much action going on.

The new bar opened with no great fanfare; a sweet, small, relaxing bar. I overheard a guy tell his companion, "Boy, these Alessio boys, they're sure tearing our little old hotel up. They're doing this and doing that. I'm sure glad they didn't change this little bar."

The building was so old, and so run down, all the upgrades ended up costing much more than we had budgeted. In many sections, the walls were two feet thick. Things we'd estimated at $4000 cost $24,000. There were other, more pleasant, surprises, too.

When we were fixing the interior sprinklers we found a large basement. Joe Coutre, who was working there, had a good idea.

"Why don't we build a walk-in freezer, and I'll buy in quantities, especially fish?" he suggested.

I had my laborers go down there to start cleaning up. Apparently, no one had been down there recently. On the section we were considering for the freezers, the doors would hardly open.

When they finally did, what a treasure trove. We discovered a cache of the most gorgeous silverware and dishes. It was quite a find. To celebrate, we threw a party for friends and dignitaries, using our newfound, antique tableware. Everyone was impressed.

We continued looking for the best spot for our walk-in. One day I got a call.

"We found something great," the foreman told me. The original owners had built an underground water reservoir. It was maybe a quarter the size of a football field, and the walls were at least seven feet thick. It was built to stay.

I looked at that built-in insulation and decided we could just put a cover on it and we'd have our walk-in freezer. It ended up saving a huge amount on our costs, both for electricity and for food, because we now could buy in bulk. We'd never been in the hotel business, so we were taking baby steps.

The Coronado building department was hard-nosed, and we had a few fights with them, but in the end, they thought the Alessios were good people. They realized we were doing our remodel right, and finally went along with us.

Meanwhile, our accountant Bob Mansfield remodeled the bookkeeping system. We had about 500 people on the payroll: janitors, gardeners, maids and so many more. It was like running a small city, and we couldn't handle it ourselves. Eventually we hired a hotel professional, Carl Lieghty, a classy guy who'd been working at the U.S. Grant Hotel downtown. That proved a wise decision.

Now Johnny could concentrate on building our clientele. The Hollywood crowd we knew from the racetrack were already regulars. When we took over the Hotel Del, Ronald Reagan, still an actor, not a politician, was a frequent guest who would come every summer. My son Larry, who was still in high school, was working at the hotel, and became pretty friendly with Reagan. The Crane family, of air conditioning fame, were also regulars, who would stay all summer and leave an extra $100,000 in our till.

But the hotel was not yet an historic monument, and hadn't yet got the national fame it later would receive. Our income varied wildly, depending on convention business, but we promoted our wonderful parties, and they brought people for longer stays.

BRIDGING THE GAP

All this happened in the early 1960s. At that time, Coronado Island was still quite isolated. There were two ways to get there from San Diego: drive south to Imperial Beach then north up the Silver Strand, or take a ferry from downtown San Diego. I loved the ferry, myself, and even though she often waited an hour or more, Mardy used to take the kids for a ride on it, when she wasn't in a hurry.

Once we owned the hotel, though, we realized we should have better access. Pat Brown was governor of California then, and we had some ties with him, but it seemed he couldn't help us. The residents of Coronado had to approve a bridge.

They didn't approve. Coronado had always been a private refuge for the Navy hierarchy, their own little haven, and they didn't welcome intruders.

We had hearings with the city of Coronado. People wanted to run the Alessios out of town. We argued that we wanted to help everyone, not just our own business, but they resisted.

"Go away and leave us alone!" they hollered. "We don't want a bridge."

Once, governor Pat Brown came to a function at the Hotel Del, and needed to get back to Los Angeles. He got caught in the back-up for the ferry. It wasn't a set-up, but it did work out that way. His eyes were opened, and finally, construction was approved.

Many people, including Pat Brown, loved getting on the ferry and coming back towards the San Diego skyline. Pat Brown, a great politician, told the Coronado residents, "The bridge is necessary for the growth and betterment of California. But if you want to keep the ferry, you won't lose your ride across the bay. "

After years of politics and negotiations, the Coronado Bridge was finally built. Pat Brown was no longer governor when it was inaugurated on August 3, 1969, and the Alessios no longer owned the Hotel Del, which we had sold to Larry Lawrence in 1963.

The first car over that spectacular span contained my brother, John Alessio, who envisioned it and fought for it for many years. Apart from the Hotel del Coronado, the sweeping span of the Coronado Bridge is the most visible and permanent Alessio contribution to the San Diego skyline, and it came about because we were so enthusiastic about promoting the Hotel Del.

Larry Lawrence was a contractor we had gotten to know through our support of the Democratic Party. He wanted the hotel and really kept on us, but we didn't think he had the financial wherewithal. We had bought the hotel for $2.5 million and put another million into it. The seven Alessio brothers decided we'd name our price and walk away with a million dollars each: $7 million.

(You may remember Larry Lawrence, who also bought the 35 acres we started off with next to the Hotel Del and put up Taco Towers there. He was a staunch Democrat, and became an ambassador during the Clinton Administration. When he passed away he was buried in Arlington National Cemetery—at least until the news leaked out that he never had served in the Navy. He's buried now in San Diego. But all that was many years later.)

Anyway, Lawrence always had a way with "other people's money" and found himself a backer who had both cash and good credit. We asked Arnie Smith to check him out, because they asked that we take back a $4 mortgage. Arnie came back with great news.

"I talked to some people and they said to let the gentleman write the check and fill in all the zeros he wants!"

We ended up with even more than the $4 million, by selling our mortgage to Arnie's Westgate Corporation, making us owners of the second largest block of stock in that diversified company: they owned U.S. National Bank, National Steel, most of the San Diego tuna fishing fleet, all the cabs in San Francisco, and countless ranches and real estate projects across the southwest.

Second largest stockholders in all that? Not too bad for a bunch of Italian boys who mostly never finished grammar school, who started off shining shoes, selling trucks, peddling meat and delivering soda. Whose parents could barely speak English, let alone read or write it. Not too bad at all. Mom and Dad would have been proud. Only in America.

CHAPTER SIXTEEN

Growing Going On

Obviously, by the early 1960s the Alessios were quite involved in the San Diego real estate market and things were going very well. We had leased offices at 4th and Broadway, and Bob Mansfield, our accountant, suggested we buy a whole block at 5th and Laurel and put up our own building. He thought we should be patient and buy it up piece by piece. It took about a year and a half, but we finally acquired the whole block. As I recall, we paid $900,000 in all for a beautiful location across the street from Balboa Park.

People told us it was too far away from downtown to compete. Financing would be the key. We hired Bird Engineering to do the architecture. They had designed a lot of our racetracks, and had helped with the Hotel Del.

By this time we brothers had a pretty good system working. Johnny took care of business south of the border, helped by Tony, Russ and the others. I was in charge of things in San Diego. So Mansfield, Bird and I drove all around California looking at buildings. We came up with some ideas and took them to the others.

Naturally, there were almost as many opinions as there were brothers; it took us almost a year to decide what to do. Looking back, I think we could have done it differently. What we did was build a monument to John Alessio and the Alessio family, because Johnny was always the dominant voice and we'd gotten used to letting him have his way.

The Alessio Building wasn't built to make a lot of money, but it was built with class. John saw to that. We covered the whole block with the first few stories, then erected an office tower, with much smaller outside dimensions, right in the middle. It looks good, but us cost a lot of rental space.

We included a huge, expensive lobby—another of Johnny's inspirations. They don't put big lobbies in office buildings anymore. They're a waste of space. Johnny hung a spectacular Mexican chandelier in the lobby, beautiful but unnecessary.

The hallways are too wide, the bathrooms too big. A lot of good space lost, but the building is certainly lovely. Now, 35 years later, we can look at it and ask, "Why did we do that? What were we thinking?"

We finally agreed on a 12-story building. Immediately, it was nicknamed "the highest building in San Diego." Not the tallest, the highest, because unlike the downtown high-rises, which start out near sea level, 5th and Laurel is in the neighborhood known as Hillcrest, overlooking the entire bay, and all the way south to Mexico and east to the mountains.

Just as we were finalizing the plans, Johnny had another brainstorm. Why not take advantage of that spectacular view by putting a restaurant on top of our office building?

Now, I don't like the restaurant business. I've seen too many fail, and I was very much against this scheme. It was probably the most serious disagreement I ever had with Russ, Tony and John. They listened politely to my reasoning, but in the end they went along with Johnny's plan. I was just a small cog in the big Alessio wheel, and I got outvoted.

When the plans were drawn up, we ran into a problem with the Federal Aviation Administration. Our building, in the flight path of incoming and outgoing air traffic at Lindbergh Field, was about two feet too high.

As always, John was determined. I don't know exactly how he did it, but in the end the FAA approved our plans, and the San Diego building department fell into line.

Now it was my job to get to work with the contractors and engineers and get the Alessio monument built. We put it out for competitive bids, and settled on the best builder in San Diego, who was coincidentally a good friend of mine, Kenneth Golden. He and his brother Robert owned Golden Construction Company, also known as M.H.Golden. They had built many of the major structures in town, and I was very comfortable with their bid. The base contract was for about $2.5million—$12 to 15 million plus in today's economy.

It turned out to be one of the nicest-looking buildings in town, and even while construction was still underway we had prospective tenants coming to us, wanting to rent space. By the time the building was done, it was more than 60 percent

Mr. A's

leased, with more people calling every day.

The Alessio brothers took the entire 11th floor. We had so many different corporations at the time we weren't sure how much space we'd need. Of course, Johnny got the first pick of offices, and chose the northwest corner, overlooking San Diego bay and Mexico. I had second choice, and decided on the southwest corner. My office was beautiful, and I was happy with it except for one thing. All the air traffic had a landing pattern that made me nervous. Sometimes I felt I should wave at the pilots, or reach out and shake their hands—the incoming planes were just that close. Eventually, though, that flight path was changed.

Unlike myself, with my beloved pastimes of hunting and travel, Johnny didn't have any real hobbies. He was happiest when remodeling. Seeing someone hammering and tearing down walls put a big smile on his face. It drove me crazy, right after we'd just built this beautiful, expensive building. But we went along with him, and the building was finally completed around 1965.

We had a grand Grand Opening. I gave a speech in front of all the invited dignitaries: the governor, state legislators, the mayor and city politicians. Another great day for the once-humble Alessio brothers.

The crowning glory of our new structure, Johnny's pet project, the restaurant on the 12th floor, was also now complete, and we named it in his honor: Mr. A's. It quickly earned a reputation as one of the top restaurants in the country. Amazingly, despite my initial reservations, after all these years and the huge influx of new restaurants in Mission

Valley, the Gaslamp Quarter, Shelter and Harbor Islands, and all around the city, Mr. A's is still going strong.

The added competition certainly cut into our profits, but we did make money, and I really can't complain.

FULL CIRCLE OF FRIENDS

We were glad to get out of the hotel business when we sold the Hotel Del. It was taking up a lot of time, and we had many irons in the fire. Still, when our loyal friend Arnie Smith called us to help him with the ailing Hotel Kona Kai on Harbor Island, we didn't turn him down. We liked to pay back the many favors he'd done us.

The Kona Kai owed Arnie a lot of money. It was located on San Diego Port Authority land, with a great setting. But it was run down, and that drove Johnny crazy. He set out planning a remodel. The Alessios gutted the hotel, then added boat slips. John did the planning, I supervised the work, the way our team always functioned. There was much to be done, but nothing near what the Hotel Del had required, and when we were done the hotel looked almost brand new.

We held onto it for a number of years, but wanted to refocus our full attention on the racing business. Arnie was aware of this and put us in touch with another friend, Lou Lipton, who owned many apartments in San Diego.

"If you boys want to sell, now would probably be a good time," Arnie recommended.

We sold it to Lipton and turned a good profit. The main benefit was that we'd done a good turn for Arnie. Good friends helping good friends, the Italian way.

I want to share a little more information on this wonderful friend, who had given us our first leg up in the world of business. C. Arnholt Smith was a self-made man, too. He wanted to own San Diego, and almost did. Once he'd built his United States National Bank into one of the biggest financial institutions in the southwest, he formed the Westgate Corporation, and took control of National Steel. Because of his connections, National Steel got almost all the ship building work on the West Coast, making wartime barges, refrigeration barges and also doing major repairs. It was a big operation.

Then Arnie started buying up fishing boats. He owned them all over the world, supplying canneries in Puerto Rico and throughout Central and South America.

He branched out into taxi cabs, eventually winning control of all the Yellow Cabs in San Francisco and Los Angeles. He owned agricultural properties, walnut farms and ranches, not necessarily the biggest money makers, but almost playthings for him.

He got involved in professional baseball. He bought the original Padre ballpark, at the foot of Broadway. He moved the Padres to the new ballpark in Mission Valley, now Qualcomm Stadium. Eventually, he sold the whole operation to McDonald's founder Ray Kroc.

During World War II, we worked together with Arnie to help out the government. Laundered money was coming to America through Mexico at that time, and it had nothing to do with dope. This was money funneled through Europe when the Allies took over small towns over there. It came back to the U.S through Mexico, and Uncle Sam had a problem with that. The government wanted to stop American currency from being accepted or used in Mexico. Johnny and Arnie came up with an idea to issue scrip to everyone crossing from the U.S. to Mexico. Arnie talked to the Department of Currency. The Mexican businesses in Tijuana weren't getting any business, just dying on the vine.

Arnie already had strong political connections; Johnny, of course, was with Banco del Pacifico. They got the deal going. We put up a little headquarters at the border crossing. People going to Mexico would stand in line and exchange their money for scrip. Merchants would accept only scrip or pesos, not dollars.

This scrip was owned by Arnie and the Alessios. It worked almost like a credit card operation. At first it was rough going: people weren't used to credit cards in those days. Eventually, though, the operation smoothed out. Tourists would spend their scrip in Mexico, the merchants would exchange the scrip at Banco del Pacifico and would pay a service charge.

Most tourists spent the scrip like Monopoly money. They'd spend much more than they planned, a bonus for the Mexican merchants. Plus, when they'd come back across the line, they'd often just keep their leftover scrip as a souvenir. This worked out for us, because we had their dollars.

We'd always worked well with Arnie Smith, because we all recognized a good opportunity when we saw it, and we knew how to share the wealth. No one got greedy. It was a win-win situation.

Unfortunately, things got tougher for Arnie around the time he sold the Padres to Ray Kroc. Arnie had a great financial empire, but when the government checked, they found he wasn't maintaining a sufficient reserve at the bank. He worked hard to get out of his financial bind, but he had made some political enemies, and that hurt him.

Ed Miller, the district attorney resented that Arnie hadn't contributed to his campaign; other political foes smelled blood and eventually, the United States National Bank was taken over. We Alessios had a major chunk of Westgate stock, but we were fortunate to get out with our $4 million intact.

We'd done a lot of deals with Arnie, but we had never seen eye to eye on politics. He was a staunch Republican, and we were loyal Democrats. We did our thing, and Arnie did his, and in the end it was politics that led to most of his undoing.

Through all of our varied enterprises, we made the acquaintance of quite a few celebrities. Down at Caliente, we got friendly not just with Elizabeth Taylor and Eddie Fisher, but my old client Bing Crosby. Victor Mature

Celebrity Cruise: (l-r) unidentified actress, Ben Gazzara, unidentified actor, Angelo, Mrs. Gazzara

was a buddy, not much of a gambler, but he liked the races, and brought some class to the track.

Mardell and I were there when Eddie Fisher opened in Las Vegas. He'd just gotten together with Liz Taylor, and he looked at Mardy, held her by the chin and told her, "You look just like my sweetheart!"

We saw Mickey Rooney frequently at Caliente. Once he was there, signing autographs for all the fans, and I walked up to him and asked, "Hey Mickey, how would you like to have mine?"

"I'd love it," he answered, straight faced. "If it's on a check."

George Raft, a genuinely humble man, would often come down with his wife, accompanied by the big band trumpeter Harry James and his wife, gorgeous Betty Grable.

In a later era, we also got friendly with the great actor, Ben Gazarra. I've still got a snapshot of him on our family boat. All our celebrity clients brought in a lot of business at Caliente, because ordinary folk would show up hoping to see a star.

Probably our closest celebrity friendship was with Ted Williams, the hall-of-famer who grew up near us when we were all kids. With the Boston Red Sox he was the last major leaguer to hit .400, and some consider him the greatest ball player ever.

I used to spend time with him, his brother and his mother, who worked for the Salvation Army. Whenever he could, Ted would play ball until sunset. When we are 15, in 1932, we both played for Hoover High. He was on the varsity, I was on the JV team.

He'd pass by our house on Polk around 5:30 or 6:00, all messed up, shirttail out, walking like he couldn't take another step. He'd always stop and say "Hi."

If I hadn't been out all day playing ball with him, it was because I had too many chores to do for my family. Ted was my friend, and my mom liked him, but she would bawl him out, half kidding, "You no good! You no good! You should helpa your mother!"

"Oh, Rose, don't worry," he'd always say. "You're gonna see my name in the papers. Big baseball player."

She didn't give up, though. That was my mom.

"Oh, you no good!" Then he'd go on home.

This went on for three or four years, same script. Finally, Ted got smart. He'd come walking down Polk, and if my mother had been baking bread, that incomparable aroma would fill the street.

Ted would come by and ask, "Rose, do I smell something? It sure smells good, Rose." And she'd go into the house, cut him a big slice and put some olive oil on it.

The "Splendid Splinter" would scarf it down like he'd never eaten before in his life. He only weighed 130 pounds when he began at Hoover High. He could have chosen to go to the old, established San Diego High School, but because he was so skinny, he thought he'd never make the team there. So he went to the new school, Hoover, with me and Bob Breitbard, who now runs the Hall of Champions in San Diego.

Ted and my mother liked each other, but she never thought he would amount to anything.

"How's a baseball player gonna make-a-money?" she'd ask. She never did understand about professional ballplayers. As we got older, it was clear he was way out of my league as a ballplayer, but we stayed pretty good friends.

Later on, when we Alessios starting doing well ourselves, and Ted was a big league star, I thought about helping other poor kids like we all were when we started. We decided to refurbish a part of Hoover High and make it into Ted Williams Field. Bob Breitbard worked out the details, and the Alessios donated $3,000 to build the field.

As the decades flew by, Ted and I maintained our friendship through

The new Ted Williams scoreboard:
(l-r) Angelo, two Hoover High Varsity players, Bob Breitbard

fishing. He loved to fish, especially for albacore. Once, when we owned the Hotel del Coronado and had a boat for entertaining guests, Ted called Breitbard and said he wanted to come fishing. Bob called me, and though our yacht wasn't really set up as a fishing boat, I was happy to do it.

When Bob called Ted, he was adamant. "It must be understood, no press, no publicity. I don't want anybody knowing what I'm doing. No photographers, nothing."

Now, we knew a lot about publicity, and we had a good friend at the *San Diego Tribune* (now the *Union Tribune*). He'd done a good job reporting on our race track, and was one of the top sports reporters on the west coast.

How he knew about this fishing trip, I don't know, but he got hold of me and said, "Angelo, I've gotta interview Ted."

"That's a no-no," I told him. "Ted said no press on the boat."

The trip wasn't scheduled till the next month, and I got to thinking. I told Johnny, "Goddamit, this guy's been such a good reporter for the race track." He always gave us great plugs. I decided we could make him look like a deckhand, and Ted would never know the difference. I told the reporter he couldn't take notes or pictures, but he could be there with us while we were all talking. He loved the idea.

Of course, our regular skipper would pilot the boat. My younger son Steven was a baseball fan, played Little League, and Ted Williams was his hero. He'd heard me talk about Ted and how we'd grown up together.

"Oh, Dad," he pleaded. "Please let me go."

And of course, I said yes.

We met Ted down on the dock, and he came aboard all smiles. On board were me, Steven, the skipper and the "deckhand" reporter. Ted was glad to see me, and we headed out to sea, catching up on everything.

I remember saying to him, "When we were kids, I bet you never thought I'd ever take you out fishing on a boat like this—one that I owned!"

"Oh yeah?" he replied. "Wanna bet?"

Ted Williams usually had something smart to say, but that really surprised me. What a compliment. I just changed the subject as we headed out to sea, but Ted always loved a friendly bet. As we got close to where the albacore were running, Ted wanted to bet he could out-fish me. I was in practice, and a pretty good fisherman by then, so I couldn't refuse.

Meanwhile, the reporter was there, making mental notes, taking everything in. He'd give me a look, and I'd want to tell Ted what was going on, but that would have ruined everything.

I think the bet was $20. We got out in the fishing grounds, and this Ted, I'm telling you, he knew how to fish. Albacore were fast and furious, and he was real good with the rod. He landed a 20-pound albacore in about four minutes, an exceptional feat. When he'd get a strike he would play the fish and wear it out. The way he would work his pole was almost like he was playing a musical instrument. A "reel" artist.

I was fighting to get the fish in at the first reel. He out-fished me. He whipped me, hands down. I heard about it for the rest of the day.

We had a great time out there, rehashing old times, talking about our old baseball coach, Mr. Caldwell. We laughed about one particular incident.

Ted was not only a brilliant hitter, but, like Babe Ruth, a good pitcher, too. Mr. Caldwell hated to use him as a pitcher, because he realized Ted's future was as a hitter. But once he really had to. He'd run out of pitchers.

It was hot as hell. Ted looked around the infield and the outfield, and waved them all into the dugout. "Come on in you guys. Cool off. I'm gonna strike this team out." And he did, he struck them out! That is one hell of a pitcher.

But then, Ted always was a cocky guy, famous for mouthing off. One time Coach got mad at him and pulled him out of the game. Hoover was losing, Ted was in the dugout, and he yelled, "Hey, Coach, if you want to win this game, you'd better put me back in."

Caldwell just walked away.

Ted kept on him. "Okay, it's up to you. If you want to lose this game, that's all right with me. Whatever you say, Coach."

Caldwell finally gave in. He put Ted back in, and we won the game. That's a star.

Anyway, the fishing trip was a success. We decided to have a big fish fry back at the Hotel Del, where Ted was staying. He invited some friends, and all the Alessios came, too. He still wolfed down his food like he hadn't eaten in weeks, just like when he was a skinny, 130 pound kid.

We'd had such a good time, Ted invited me to come bonefishing with him in Florida. When I finally could make it out there, he could not, but he arranged for one of the best guides to go with me. Though I'm not an experienced bone fisherman, it was a truly exciting experience.

But the whole time I was fishing in Florida, I couldn't help thinking about Ted Williams and me, playing baseball till there was no more light, coming home disheveled and dog tired, and my mom stuffing her fresh bread in our faces. How things had changed.

The Hotel Del Cabin Cruiser – Miss Caliente

Part IV

Personal Notes About
the Author & His Family

CHAPTER SEVENTEEN

Travels with Mardy

I'm getting close to finishing the story of the Alessio brothers and all the good fortune that came our way. I've also talked quite a bit in this book about Mardy and me—how we met and courted and finally got married many, many years ago. I've even mentioned a little from time-to-time about our own family—Mardy's and mine—and our children. That's one thing I'm really the most proud of—my wife and children. And none of it would have been possible without Mardy at my side.

Everyone who knows me, knows I'm a great kidder. That's what I do and it puts a smile on people's faces, and I like that. Making people laugh comes naturally, but the hard thing for me is to be serious and nice at the same time. I just never have been very good at it. But I have to say that the key to whatever success I've achieved has been because of Mardy. Next year she and I will celebrate our 63rd wedding anniversary. Now that's really amazing—especially these days when people marry and divorce quicker than they buy a new car.

One of the secrets to our marriage has been our homes. They've always been warm and comfortable—where people could feel relaxed, yet special. Mardy made all that happen. She's kind of a magician when it comes to that sort of thing. Always has been.

Of all the Alessio brothers, I was the one who most loved to travel. When I started making good money, I told Mardell we were going to see the world. Logically enough, she asked me, "Who's going to take care of our three kids?"

"I don't know."

"Well, I'm not going to leave them," she said

"I'll see you when I get back, then."

But it always ended up that when I was ready to leave, she had her bags packed. We would leave the kids with her mother.

Of course, we had our wonderful vacation home in Puerto Vallarta. Once it was finished, we went all out finding Mexican knick-knacks to fill it with. That was fun. Puerto Vallarta wasn't yet the big tourist town it is today, and the stores didn't really have displays. You'd have to "discover" what you wanted, like a treasure hunt. Mardy would go into the back room and emerge with great finds. We even went over to Guadalajara, to find some special china.

The house was finished and decorated with Mardy's special flair. We had a vacation home to be proud of, and the kids had a ball there. When Elizabeth Taylor bought a house there during the filming of "Night of the Iguana," we'd wave to her on the street, and got to know her as a neighbor.

Once we visited her house down the street, a nice older house, but sloppily done, compared to ours. In those days, you could go from one end of town to the other in about eight minutes. Once word got around that Liz lived there, the whole town started booming. It was sad to see that happen, but we adjusted.

We met a young lady who lived nearby, Darrien. Her two daughters went to school with Lee Iacocca's girls, and eventually Lee and Darrien started dating and then married. Back in San Diego, Lee came to town to deliver a speech, and he and Darrien came into Mr. A's and dined with us.

That Puerto Vallarta house was one of the craziest moves I ever made, yet everything about it was filled with excitement and surprises. I guess that's why we loved it so.

Thinking back, I don't remember learning much in school. Maybe

Dinner at Mr. A's: (l-r) Lee Iacoca,
Baron O'Brien, Mardy, Angelo,
Darien (Puerto Vallarta neighbor)

that's why I loved traveling and seeing the world. When we were on a trip I'd wake up and tell Mardell, "Get up honey; we've got to go to school today."

We started with a trip to the Fiji Islands, Bali, and Singapore. Then we tackled Europe. One of our first European adventures was to San Giovanni in Fiore in the Cosenza province of southern Italy, where my parents had grown up and married so long ago. It's still a very poor and isolated area. We had to take a cogwheel train to get up into the mountains.

It was a real trip back in time. The people wore traditional costumes, and if you wanted to take a snapshot the women would turn and run away. We didn't have any close relations living there, but we did have a cousin. As the postmaster, he made $28 a month, and was a bigshot.

The people were very poor, but sweet. I'd often wondered where the Alessio brothers had gotten their drive. After seeing where our parents had come from, I concluded it must be genetic. Imagine what our parents went through to leave this tiny village with no money, head down those hills, get on a ship and come to America. They had to be hard workers.

Later we went to India for about three weeks; that was lovely. We went all over Spain. We went to Africa, once on a tour, other times on safari, and brought back magnificent trophies. We visited Sweden, and Russia, and went hunting in Alaska.

One crazy trip was up the Amazon River. We started out by sailing down the Caribbean on the Alcoa Line. I'll never forget that cruise, because I got to see Mardy in her first bikini. We went to Bogota and boarded an old, unbelievably scary plane which took us to an old boat once used to ship rubber.

It carried two classes of passenger. There were just three of us in first class. Below us were the Amazon natives, traveling from one village to another with their kids, chickens and goats, cooking their own meals. A whole different world.

We'd approach each village, and the boat would blow its whistle, and the natives would come out to the dock with trinkets. They didn't use currency, but you could trade little mirrors, razor blades, chocolates and pick up some beautiful native crafts. I bought myself a blowgun, but never got any good with it.

We'd have cocktails at sunset, and let the jungle noises lull us to sleep. On Mother's Day, I took Mardy out in a little canoe to go alligator hunting with a spotlight. Our guide would spot these little, footlong alligators, grab them by the tail and bring them into the boat for a minute, then throw them back in. That was our alligator hunt.

A really different trip was when we flew on the Concorde to Morocco for a week. Very luxurious, and of course, fast. I think the flight from New York to Morocco took all of five hours, during

Angelo and Mardy on vacation in Egypt

which they kept feeding us some of the best French food I've ever tasted. In Morocco we were treated like royalty, literally walking on rose petals!

We took a trip to China, when you could only travel in a group. The most outstanding part was the cruise up the Yangtze River on a ship once owned by an emperor.

That was not our first trip to the far east. My brother John was responsible for that one. He came up with a brainstorm that had unexpected benefits.

Up until 1950 or so, jockeys had a really rough ride. Too many racing deaths and permanent injuries occurred when jockeys would fall off and be trampled by pounding hooves. We didn't like to see that happen, and Johnny thought, "Why don't we design a helmet like policemen wear?"

The helmet would have to be sturdy but lightweight, because the jockeys often got their "ride" based on total pounds.

Johnny experimented with several materials and finally came up with one he liked. We started using it at Caliente, and the Jockey Guild was ecstatic. They flew Johnny to their New York headquarters and named him their "Man of the Year." That helmet was a real lifesaver.

Because of his patented invention, John became world famous with jockeys and race track owners. As a result of his helmet, insurance rates for horse tracks dropped dramatically, because deaths and injuries were cut in half.

We didn't do it to make money, though, we were trying to save lives. Suddenly the Alessios were heroes to jockeys all over the world. We got some serious inquiries from Australia and Japan; they wanted us to introduce our helmets there.

I was the only Alessio who really loved to travel, so Johnny offered me the opportunity. Our PR man at Caliente, Ken Bojens, arranged the trip for me and Mardell.

The Australians were very businesslike, and were relieved when I told them they could use the helmet without paying a royalty. Johnny and I had agreed the helmet was strictly for the health of the jockeys and the betterment of racing.

In Japan, we had a radically different experience. We were met at the airplane with a big limousine, and men bowing at us. None of them spoke English, except the "interpreter" who was really more of a travel guide.

They checked us into one of the finest hotels in Tokyo and told us we'd have a luncheon for the press and everyone interested in the helmet.

In their tradition, I got all the attention; they acted as if Mardy wasn't even there, though I could see they were checking her out. The luncheon was at the Jockey Guild building, and Mardy wasn't invited.

The luncheon was hilarious. The head table was set for 20 people, and I sat there with a translator. I tried to talk with hand gestures.

They set some food in front of me and told me, "Eat, eat!" No one else had any food. I later learned this was a great honor. After I made my presentation, everyone came up and bowed some more. I felt like General MacArthur.

The translator invited me up to the fourth floor for a Tokyo bath. I'd heard of these, and it did sound like fun. So after more pictures and talk, I went up in the elevator and was met by two of the tiniest, cutest Japanese girls I'd ever seen. They welcomed me and led me to the steam room, directing me with hand signals where to go and what to do.

I got undressed, and ready for my bath, and started getting real concerned. They were so cute in their tiny bikinis, smiling all the time. I came out with a towel, and stepped into the big bath, and they started washing me.

They worked on my shoulders with sweet smelling soap, all very tender. You can imagine what I'm thinking. They were washing me and doing a great job.

Finally, they got down to my private parts, and handed me a wash rag and soap and said, "You finish?"

I finished, and they wrapped me in a big robe and brought me over to a massage table. They both gave me a heavenly massage; one even walked on my back. I was in orbit.

Back at the hotel, Mardell insisted, "Tell me what happened!"

"I feel like I'm on cloud nine," I said, and told her the whole story.

That evening, our hosts invited me to the theater. They never mentioned my wife. I was hoping she was included and thankfully she was. A bellman had told her there would be a party for us both at a fancy Japanese opera. When we arrived, again I got the bowing and VIP treatment, while Mardy got nothing but sideways glances. But it turned out to be a fine evening for both of us. The Japanese had hospitality for men down to a science.

Tony and I were the only brothers who really enjoyed hunting; Mardy would go only if the weather was warm. I hunted polar bear out of Nome, Alaska and got one big enough for the record book—13 and a half feet from nose to tail. The bearskin rug is still in my house. On another trip I shot a 2500 pound Kodiak bear.

Over the years I was able to build a major trophy collection: black bear, Dall sheep, and moose from Alaska; jaguar from British Honduras; tiger from India; elephant from Africa. These trips were great adventures, but now of course many of these species are endangered, and those trips are in the past.

By 1982 Mardy and I had seen most of the world, but not too much of our own country. We bought a 33-foot motor home, an Imperial Holiday Rambler, everything deluxe. We started traveling, and I kept a map in my office, all zigzagged with the routes we had taken. We must have crossed half a dozen times from the West Coast to the East and back. Then we started going north and south. On some of our trips we'd be gone a month, and after seeing the rest of the world, I must say the good old USA looked pretty good to us.

We took a long trip all the way up Highway 101 to British Columbia, then drove up the inside passage from Vancouver. It was the fall, and very beautiful. We'd already been to Alaska, so we headed east, then south, stopping in many Canadian towns. We crossed Canada, and into the U.S. near Niagara Falls.

We had a lot of fun in that motor home. I bought a little Chevette and towed it along, so we could park in a campground and drive out to see the sights. Outdoor Resorts of America had the nicest parks, with hookups and cable TV, and we met a lot of good people in those campgrounds.

Mardy loved to cook, and we had some of her best meals ever in that motor home. Driving around the U.S. was great: we were on our own, we didn't need a guide. We did just what we wanted to every day.

Back in San Diego, I was reading the paper one morning and I saw this big ad on this new condo complex with a health center, and a sort of a semi-small hospital. Not that I figured we needed that, but I felt it looked pretty good. It was in La Jolla overlooking the ocean and Mexico, just a fabulous view. I went and took a look; it was only about five years old.

It's 21 stories high and faces the Mormon Tabernacle which is a beautiful sight, lit up every night. On the 20th floor there are four semi-penthouses; they're all about 2500 square feet.

There was one unit on the southwest corner with a beautiful glassed-in veranda. Mardy decided this was the one, so we bought it and again she came through with the decorating. I'll tell you, she did a great job and we got to use a lot of our old furniture. I got to bring my big polar bear out and put it in our living room. It felt like home. It's got two bedrooms and a living room, dining room, nice kitchen, and two bathrooms.

The place has everything you could ever want—a beautiful restaurant, wide hallways, big lobby, valet service, room service, housekeeping, library, nice gym—you name it. The help is nice and all the people there are friendly. It still took me a little while to adjust myself, I would say maybe eight months. I just had to change a lot of my old ways. The people there were terrific, I got to like them; they were all just great people and I figured now I've got a new big family. I lost my old family because they grew up, and now I move into this big family, and they're very nice people—generals and colonels, and judges.

It's working out great, really, I like it; I don't miss the yard, I don't miss the gardener, I don't miss the broken water pipes or calling the plumber.

Only in America could this happen to a guy like me—an Italian kid with little education and nothing going for him but hard work, good parents, six great brothers, and one special wife.

CHAPTER EIGHTEEN

The Next Generation

My brothers are gone now, but I think it's fair to say that the first generation of American Alessios left its mark, both in the U.S. and in Mexico. We had always had mutually respectful relations with the people of our neighbor country, and we had certainly contributed to its economy.

We employed hundreds of Mexicans at Caliente, but we knew there was more to do. What did the children have to look forward to? We wanted to give them hope for a better future.

Although our dad had been in poor health for much of his life, and our mom never brought home a paycheck, we Alessios always had our hopes and dreams, and one of the things that made us hopeful was the American school system. Yes, my older brothers had quit school to go to work early in their lives, but school was free, and as we younger brothers grew up, mandatory. Hard work and education were the keys to success.

In 1968, we began to build schools in Tijuana, one of the best things we ever did. We picked poor areas where the city couldn't afford

to build schools, and we were given permission to name the schools after our father. Dominic number one, two, three, all the way up to eleven. We promised the city we'd turn over the schools outfitted with everything

One of the Alessio school openings: (l-r front) Rubin Bejarano, a Governor of Baja, Mardy, Angelo, John

down to the chalk for the boards, and they promised to maintain them in the same condition.

It was grand to see the looks on the people's faces as construction progressed. It seemed like Christmas morning, every day. We built quality schools, full-sized, well-constructed buildings. Of course, I was in charge. At the time, each school cost about $75,000—close to a million in today's dollars.

We set up a department to work the schools, as if it were our own school district. The reaction on the streets was incredible. Children and parents would come up, kneel down and kiss our shoes. They'd cry and hug us. Man, I don't care how rich you are, or how tough, when that happens, you've got to cry, too. And I did.

These were some of the most touching moments in my life. Each school opened with much fanfare; military officers, the mayor, often the governor would be there. The Alessio brothers would all speak, Mardell and the other wives would cut the ribbons.

Later, both in Tijuana and San Diego, people would tell us, "If it wasn't for your schools, I don't know what I would have done."

Once at the Whaling Bar, a popular La Jolla watering hole, I walked in without a dinner reservation. They told me it would be a half hour wait. Five minutes later, while we were waiting in the bar, a little Mexican guy came up and announced, "Mr. Alessio, your table is ready."

It was Manny, the maitre d'hotel. When I stood up, he told me, with tears in his eyes, "Mr. Alessio, thank you, thank you. If it hadn't been for your school, I wouldn't have this job!" My eyes were wet, too.

Incidents like that happened more times than I can count, and they continue to this day.

One other thing we did for the kids of Tijuana was to throw a big Christmas party every year. The tradition started out small in 1960, as a Christmas celebration for the orphans. Eventually it grew to be a party for 10,000 of the very poorest citizens

It became a great social event. All the poorest kids and their families wanted to be at the Alessio Christmas party. Through the years it kept growing. Finally, we had to have the Army come in and take charge of traffic. We'd spend the whole year getting ready, and we made a pledge to the Mexicans and ourselves that we would throw the biggest Christmas party in the whole country.

Everyone helped out. Taxi drivers donated time, and buses too. We hired a guy to buy carloads of gifts in the U.S. The first kids to receive their gifts were the crippled, blind, and dying. After that, they lined up by age. We tried to give every little girl a doll, every boy a baseball and bat. Each child got a big bag of tortillas and Mexican staples, so the whole family could have a Christmas dinner.

We tried to work it out so everyone would leave our party with a smile on their face. The Army band would play, dignitaries came to distribute gifts. Arnie Smith was there once, with tears running down his face; Governor Pat Brown, too. Some of our Hollywood friends from the track would help. Everyone wept with joy at the sight of those happy young faces. It really put everyone in the Christmas spirit.

Of course, we had our own children to think about. Louie never married, but between the rest of us six brothers we had 25 kids. Mardy and my first child was our daughter Rosalie, now married to Bill O'Brien, with five children of their own. Bill is a wonderful guy, a businessman and part owner of a manufacturing company, very successful.

As a first-time Italian father, I confess I was a little disappointed that my first-born was a girl. I wanted a son to carry on the family name. But Rosalie and I were very tight; she was a feisty gal, with a mind of her own. She was pretty and popular, and boys chased after her in packs, but I kept a close eye on her. It was tough on Mardy and me when she was a teenager.

She was good in school, and decided to go to the University of southern California, where she joined a sorority. By that time, the Alessio name was well known, and I was doing very well. When people asked her what her father did, she'd tell them, "He sells trucks."

Once she was away in school, we got along much better. The first time I went to visit her, she ran down the stairs of the sorority house, crying "Daddy, Daddy!"

She picked out Bill before she even met him. She really pursued him, a big football star, and soon she brought him home to meet the folks. By then, we were living in a big, expensive house, with a tennis court and a pool. I was afraid he'd take one look and think she was some kind of heiress.

When they started talking about marriage, they asked for my approval. I gave it, but I told them they should both stay in school.

Rosalie and Bill O'Brien on their wedding day.

Rosalie wanted to have a baby, so I made sure that Bill could finish school, and when the wedding came, it was a beautiful thing. We still owned the Hotel Del, the renovations were complete, and we put on a fabulous wedding in the ballroom.

Bill was still in school when Rosalie delivered our first grandchild, Bret O'Brien. For a while, when things were tough for the new mother, Mardy would fly up to L.A. and help out. When Bill graduated, they came down to San Diego, and Bill came to work for me at International. A few years later, he came on safari with me and Rosalie's brother Larry, my first son. That was a great trip.

Larry also went to USC, and later to Hastings Law School in San Francisco. He's in the family business, one-third owner of Alessio Leasing, does all my legal work, and also works for the Alessio Corporation. He also has great kids, Laura, and my namesake Angelo, who was born on my own birthday.

Our younger son is Steven. He was the athlete of the family, went out for basketball and baseball, but football was his favorite. He went to the University of Arizona, a nice school but with a reputation as a party school. When we owned the track in Tucson, I met some of his professors, and they promised to keep an eye on him for me.

They did a good job. Steve graduated and joined the family business while Larry was still in law school. He also owns a third of Alessio Leasing. With his easy-going personality, he was

Steve Alessio

a natural for "accounts receivable"—people would pay their rent checks just because he made them laugh. He married the daughter of one of our tenants, Christy, and they've got a daughter, Emily. Steve dotes on her.

So the Alessio name is perpetuated, and our family, as always, still works together. Who would ever believe our journey? I can hardly believe it myself, and I was there.

Larry Alessio

Index

SUNBELT PUBLICATIONS
"Adventures in the Natural and Cultural History of the Californias"
Series Editor—Lowell Lindsay

San Diego Series:
Rise and Fall of San Diego: 150 Million Years...Abbott
Only in America: The Story of the Alessio Brothers..Alessio
More Adventures with Kids in San Diego..Botello, Paxton
Cycling San Diego, 3rd Edition..Copp, Schad
La Jolla: A Celebration of Its Past..Daly-Lipe
A Good Camp: Gold Mines of Julian and the Cuyamacas..Fetzer
San Diego Mountain Bike Guide...Greenstadt
San Diego Specters: Ghosts, Poltergeists, Tale...Lamb
San Diego Padres, 1969-2001: A Complete History ....Papucci
San Diego Architecture (SDAF)..Sutro
Campgrounds of San Diego County ....Tyler

Southern California Series:
Gateway to Alta California: Expedition to San Diego, 1769..................................Crosby
Portrait of Paloma: A Novel ....Crosby
Warbird Watcher's Guide to the Southern California Skies..Smith
Campgrounds of Santa Barbara and Ventura Counties..Tyler
Campgrounds of Los Angeles and Orange Counties ....Tyler
Mission Memoirs:Reflections on California's Past...Ruscin
California's El Camino Real and Its Historic Bells ....Kurillo, Tuttle
Orange County: A Photographic Collection...Hemphill

California Desert Series:
Anza-Borrego A To Z: People, Places, and Things...D.Lindsay
The Anza-Borrego Desert Region (Wilderness Press)..Lindsay
Palm Springs Oasis: A Photographic Essay ....Lawson
Desert Lore of Southern California, 2nd Ed...Pepper
Peaks, Palms, and Picnics:Day Journeys Coachella Valley..Pyle
California Desert Miracle: Parks and Wilderness..Wheat

Baja California Series:
The Other Side: Journeys in Baja California...Botello
Cave Paintings of Baja California, Rev. Ed. ....Crosby
Backroad Baja: The Central Region ....Higginbotham
Lost Cabos: The Way it Was (Lost Cabos Press) ....Jackson
Journey with a Baja Burro ....Mackintosh
Houses of Los Cabos (Amaroma)...Martinez, ed.
Mexicoland: Stories from Todos Santos (Barking Dog Press)...................................Mercer
Baja Legends: Historic Characters, Events, Locations...Niemann
Loreto, Baja California (Tio Press)..O'Neil
Baja Outpost: The Guestbook from Patchen's Cabin..Patchen
Sea of Cortez Review ....Redmond